just walking the dogs

just walking the dogs

joe bennett

HAZARD PRESS
publishers

To my mother, Joy

All the articles in this book were first published between
April 1997 and August 1998 in the Christchurch *Press* or the
Wellington *Evening Post* or the *New Zealand Herald.*
The author would particularly like to thank Bruce Rennie
of the *Press* for his encouragement and perception.

First published 1998
Reprinted 1998
Copyright © 1998 Joe Bennett

The author asserts his moral rights in the work.

ISBN 1-877161-49-7

Published by Hazard Press
P.O. Box 2151, Christchurch, New Zealand
Front cover photograph by Reg Graham
Cover design by John Burt
Production and design by Orca Publishing Services Ltd
Printed by Spectrum Print Ltd, Christchurch

CONTENTS

Introduction

I have had it easy. I was born into the middle classes of southern England in April 1957. Precisely three months later, Harold Macmillan told my parents that they had never had it so good.

I have not fought. I have not suffered. Prosperity and peace deprived me of everything that gives a childhood zing. I was fed, loved and happy. I did not have to go to church or learn the piano. My father never lost his job, nor my mother her temper. I was only mildly molested by my cricket coach. I went to a good school, and a better university where I drank almost as much as was good for me.

Since then jobs have fallen into my lap. Lovers haven't, but when I stopped crying I found I didn't much mind. Though I have travelled timidly my address has always been Easy Street.

If anything holds these articles together it is that I like people but not in herds. I distrust all beliefs, most thought and anything ending in ism. Most opinion is emotion in fancy dress.

Language seduces me. I can sniff in the following pages the influence of numerous authors, most of whom hold strong opinions. When I read Evelyn Waugh I agree with him. But when I read Orwell, O'Rourke, Amis, Austen or the King James Bible I agree with them too. It is not their opinions I believe, it is their style.

Most of these articles began as vague ideas or single sentences. As I wrote, the ideas changed. Sometimes the original sentence disappeared. What emerged often surprised me. If the words rang right or made me laugh I let them stay. As the little girl said, 'How do I know what I think till I see what I say?'

When I got stuck I took the dogs for a walk.

Old Stoaty

It's love, you see. When I paid $16-something today instead of the $15 I paid yesterday for fifty cigarettes to get me through the morning, I did so, as you would imagine, with a smile on my lips and a song in my heart. 'Oh, Mr Treasury Man,' went the song, 'whip me, hurt me, punish me and scourge me, for I must sin no more.'

What's so lovely about the tax increase on cigarettes is the thought that it comes from the heart. Down there in Wellington there's a stoat-eyed civil servant with bad breath, slip-on shoes and a suit of impeccable anonymity who cares about me. This is the story of his love.

In his bid to save my life my stoaty little lover is prepared to put aside all economic reasoning . He will ignore the truth that if I pop off after fifty years of smoking I will have paid enough tax to buy the hospital I pop off in. He will ignore the truth that if I pop off a bit early, as is the habit of smokers, I won't be toddling to the post office *post mortem* to pick up a couple of decades of pension which I have paid for. No, his love for me is such that, even though it is utterly unjustified by any statistical measure, he will break the habit of his rumbustious life of accountancy and tax me anyway.

It's not just the money either. Old Stoaty knows I am a sinner. He has seen me huddled in the sleet outside the front door of a dinner party with a group of other lost souls, and he has heard us laughing while those within have sat in anal-retentive restraint over the taramasalata. Stoaty has seen the non-smokers drift in ones and twos to join the knot of sinful smokers until suddenly it's an outdoors party and things are humming. Stoaty has seen, and Stoaty knows it is a very bad thing.

Stoaty knows too the siren voices that tempt me to sin again. 'No pleasure is worth giving up for two more years in a rest-home,' said the great tempter Kingsley Amis. As Stoaty knows, the time will come when I shall lust after life in a rest-home with a room slightly larger than my bed and no visitors and brutal nurses and boiled vegetables and indoor bowls and community singing and incontinence and bewilderment and a rapturous weekly minibus trip to the shopping mall which I won't remember. But I will remember Stoaty. Every morning at bedpan time, O Stoaty, I shall remember you.

For Stoaty knows, and I must learn, that it is my duty to live as long as possible. When salt is thought to be bad for me I must eat no salt. When next year it is thought to be good for me I must eat it a lot. I must eat low-fat spreads that taste of petrol and read *Consumer* magazine. I must learn that tomorrow matters more than today and that taking out life insurance is not like betting on a horse with no legs, but rather a sensible option.

Booze is out. Joy is out. Above all fags are out, for to see the look on the face of a smoker when he sips the first of his day's forty coffees and draws on that first cigarette is to look on the face of the damned.

I guess that at the crux of it I must realise that at forty-one I am still a child, and like a child I cannot make decisions for myself and I must look to Stoaty in all things.

George Orwell understood. 'Old Stoaty is watching you,' he said. It's love, you see.

Tools for men

At this time of the year it is important to rake up leaves. If you leave them lying, nature will rot them down into something useful. Since gardening is the art of messing nature around, that obviously will not do.

Today I saw a man attacking a pile of leaves with a thing that looked like an elephant's head with an engine. The engine roared, smoke billowed, and if he jammed the monstrous nozzle hard up against the leaves they rustled a bit. It was perhaps the most useless machine I have seen; and as soon as I saw it I wanted one.

In many ways it resembled a water-blaster. Any job a water-blaster does can be done in half the time with a scrubbing brush. But for a man a water-blaster beats a scrubbing brush every time because it's great for practical jokes and the opposite of a prostate problem.

Every tool, you see, has a job to do. That job is to confer status. Turn up at a working bee in a leather builder's apron with a battered 24-ounce claw hammer dangling from the hip like a Colt 45 and people will see you as a man who knows. And as a man who knows you are entitled to spend the working bee drinking beer, giving advice, saying 'noggin' a lot and lending out your 24-ounce claw hammer to stop it bruising your hip.

Jack-hammers, concrete mixers, road-drills – indeed all tools that require the use of ear-muffs – are desirable additions to the toolshed. Ear-muffs, of course, are not. Hearing is dispensable; status isn't.

Every man should also own a circular saw. It makes you screw your eyes up so you look like Clint Eastwood. Furthermore, no saw can match it when it comes to cutting through nails. There's something about the scream of metal on metal and the sheen of a well-halved nail that sings to a man's soul.

No man, however, buys a cordless rechargeable drill. He may be given such a drill for Christmas, but on Boxing Day he takes it to the builders' merchants as a down-payment on a real drill with double chuck, hammer action and a cable like a fat black snake. Such a drill has two handles so that it can and must be fired from the hip like an M16.

Nevertheless, when handled properly almost any machine can become a good thing. For an example, as well-known man P.J. O'Rourke has observed, take the vacuum cleaner.

A man with a vacuum cleaner just has to discover exactly what the vacuum cleaner will suck up. Paper clips rattle nicely up the pipe. Full ashtrays are fun. A merry gentleman of my acquaintance burned the guts out of three consecutive vacuum cleaners by cleaning out the grate with them. I admire that. He convinced the manufacturers to replace the first one. The second two he claimed on insurance. I admire that even more.

All the same, when vacuuming, one should resist the goldfish bowl.

The most important man's machine is, of course, his car. Men need a Honda Civic; men want a Ferrari. A man's car has a short gearstick with a wooden knob, two seats, no boot and an acre of bonnet. The bonnet has the same psychological effect on men as the nozzle on the leaf-blower. On the distant tip of the bonnet is an upstanding bit of chrome in the shape of the maker's logo. This is circular so the driver can use it like a rifle-sight.

Beyond even the car is the nuclear ICBM. These have sadly gone out of fashion except in manly India, but ordinary missiles will do, too. Exocets, Sidewinders, Silkworms, Scuds – they're serious men's machines. They shift leaves.

The soul of the city

As the sage once said, 'the soul of any city is its park'. That sage knew his onions.

There's a drunk. At six o'clock on a Saturday morning in winter he shambles out of one of those exquisite concrete bunkers that dot North Hagley Park and heads for somewhere else. Through the darkness he bears an indescribable bundle and he grunts as he goes.

At the same frozen hour a tribe of scrawnies leap from their Merivale beds of Danish wooden slats. They pull on cutaway shorts and training shoes with a swoosh on the side and more technology in the sole than a Ford Cortina. Across Carlton Mill Road they bounce and into the frozen park. The drunk grunts.

An eerie half-light begins to wake the ducks. Round and round the park the scrawnies run, their scything legs like those anatomical skinless maps in podiatrists' surgeries. On their faces the mask of grim endeavour. The drunk does not acknowledge them. They do not acknowledge the drunk.

The sun peeps. It drives away the serious scrawnies, sends them bounding back to muesli and that green milk that has had the milk taken out. Their place on the running tracks is taken by the gaspies.

The gaspies are mostly male and mostly on doctor's orders. They do not like to run. Their shorts are sad things, the remnants of beach fashions from the seventies or from rugby when you could kick for touch from outside the twenty-five. The gaspies' only pleasure in running is stopping. They have little pumpkin bellies. Sometimes dogs accompany them. The dogs lean on trees smoking while their owners catch them up. As the gaspies pass each other, they smile the sort of smile that torture victims favour.

The sun is warming to its task. Enter the large women. The large women come in pairs. They wear weatherproof make-up and costly track suits. As they walk, they swing their arms as if trying to clear jungle. They also talk. And they have dogs which trot daintily but don't swing their arms. The large women exude happiness, but in due course, as the sun thaws the turf, the large women give way to the tiny sporties.

The tiny sporties wear rugby jerseys which they will grow into within a couple of decades. From a distance the tiny sporties look like little tents with feet. They don't play rugby; they play swarming. Somewhere in the swarm there may or may not be a ball. Every so often a rogue tiny sporty will break away from the swarm and score a try. It is the second half, so the tiny scores at the wrong end. There are tears. Mothers whose tracksuits testify to the elasticity of nylon envelope their offspring.

As the sun climbs the sky, the tiny sporties become medium-sized sporties with haircuts that look like accidents. The medium-sizers don't play swarming; they play swearing. But having sworn they too move on, taking their hair and vocabulary to McDonald's. They are replaced by the big and the serious, the ones who have at last grown into their rugby jerseys.

For eighty minutes of winter afternoon the park shudders and thunders. Then a whistle, cheers, and bedraggled dirty men head for an evening of beer and lics, leaving only a litter of insulation tape to clog the council mowers on the Monday morning.

The winter sun lowers. The air chills. Mothers with pushchairs flee the stretching shadows. A few scrawnies nip out for a last burst of scrawny relish. Night seeps into the spaces. The ducks swivel their heads into the world's least comfortable sleeping position. Knots of party-goers straggle through the park, pushing, laughing, loud in the great black silence.

Night has settled. The sexually dubious melt among the trees. Vandals push over the rugby posts. The Securicor car cruises with its floodlight, illuminating trees with criminal tendencies. Then in its unforgiving beam it snares a stooped and shambling figure coming from somewhere else. The figure grunts and bears his bundle towards a concrete bunker.

The soul of the city sleeps.

The bathroom floor

You may not have heard about it, but twenty years ago today I was thrown out of a squalid little flat in Spain for refusing to wash the bathroom floor. My argument, which I thought, and still think, a strong one, was that it would only get dirty again.

Since then I have learned that, for a man, keeping the bathroom clean is easy. You pay someone else to do it. If you can't afford that, you get married. It amounts, in the end, to much the same thing.

Keeping the body clean is less easy. I suppose you could pay someone else to do it, but if you pause to imagine only a cloth between the cleaning lady and your coccyx, you head for the shower alone.

The first law of the shower states that no two shower controls in the universe are the same. The second states that the temperature markings on shower controls bear no relation to the temperature of the water. The third states that, however much a shower control may rotate, the degree of rotation required to change from ice-cold to scalding is never more than one millimetre.

Years of research and millions of dollars have gone into perfecting a plastic that grips nicely when dry but is slippery when wet. It is used to make shower tubs. It kills people. They slip, they shatter a hip and pain immobilises them. In falling, however, they have jolted the shower control just over a millimetre.

What they needed, of course, was a rubber bathmat with vaguely obscene little suckers underneath, like the tips of those arrows that boys lick and then fire at windows and girls. Such arrows never stick but they are a satisfying means of distributing saliva.

Rubber bathmats, on the other hand, do stick to shower tubs. But peel one off – and what a deeply sexy noise that makes – and look underneath. What you're looking at is the birthplace of the

Ebola virus. Penicillin doesn't come into it. This stuff's black. With feelers.

With showers so perilous, ordinary baths remain understandably popular. In the nineteenth century when people were smaller, baths were bigger. Now we're bigger, they're smaller. It's called progress. Submerge the shoulders in a modern bath and your knees rise like twin Krakatoas.

The first rule of the bath is that it is impossible to position one's head satisfactorily at the tap end. Go to the other end, however, and there's the problem of how to get more hot water into the bath without sitting up. The sort of toes we need got left behind somewhere in the climb out of evolution's swamp.

Taps on the side of the bath are not the answer. Baths are supposed to induce relaxation. It's hard to relax when the hot tap is gaping so close to your crotch that there's only a washer between you and a skin-graft.

Baths, however, are splendid for some things. The first of these is smoking, because a bath is a ready-made and efficient ashtray. They're also good for reading in – but not library books. Rule two of the bath is that library books fall into it. Rule three is all other books do, too.

The only other source of water in the bathroom is the hand-basin, easily identifiable by the stains beneath the taps and the build-up of crud in the soap-holder that doesn't hold onto the soap. Hand-basins have uses, especially when the toilet's occupied, but they are not places to wash. Washing oneself at a hand-basin is simply a means of transferring water from a bowl to the floor.

Which, if I had only realised it at the time, would have solved my little Spanish problem rather neatly.

Beds

The recipe for good sleep is a bed and a clear conscience. Either ingredient can be replaced by gin. Gin has always been gin, and a clean conscience is still available to anyone who doesn't sell real estate, but beds have changed.

I had thought that a bed was anything horizontal and softer than the ground, but I thought wrong. Beds have become a mirror of the times. Whoever coined the name Beds R Us may not have been able to spell but he knew a thing or two.

The bed of the eighties was the waterbed. Waterbeds had something. That something was smut. Waterbeds were the great blousy whores of the bedding world; men liked them more than women did because they imagined romping in them. The makers of waterbeds knew that. They decked the frames in brothel velvet, and they padded and buttoned the headboards. In effect waterbeds were built of flesh, taut, tumescent and tactile.

When first I got the chance to sleep on a waterbed I was drunk. I found that whenever I moved, little ripples radiated outwards through the mattress. Then the little ripples radiated back. On the way they met more little ripples heading outwards. My head bobbed like a dinghy. Nausea rose. Suddenly I had no choice; I had to sit upright.

The scientific name for this sensation, incidentally, is 'the whirling pits', and at university I learned the cure: keep one foot on the floor. If you're drunk enough to get the whirling pits then you're drunk enough to sleep with one foot on the floor. In my day you got a real education at varsity.

But the waterbed was not just smut and ripples. It was also a womb. It cradled the sleeper like amniotic fluid.

In the frozen winter of 1991 I slept for three months in a

waterbed beside tall windows overlooking Hagley Park. It was, I suppose, a womb with a view. Every morning I looked out from the warm embrace of water at the white expanse of park; every morning I had to wrench myself from under the covers and into the cruel air. I understood why babies wail when they are born.

Six years ago you could buy a sexy three-tonne womb in every street in town. Waterbed City competed with Waterbed World competed with Wet Dreams Inc. Then suddenly the voluptuous eighties gave way to the Kate Moss nineties, and the womb-boom burst.

There is, they say, no accounting for taste, but clearly a herd-instinct lingers in the human mind. The typically melodious German word for it is *zeitgeist*, but I wonder if there is perhaps some term in physics to describe the sudden switch of polarity that took us in no time from the self-indulgence of the waterbed to the flimsiness of the futon.

The Japanese have always been minimalists. They cook fish minimally and grow minimal bonsai trees. They make wonderful minimal soups garnished with a single sliver of mushroom. They have, I am told, railway hotels that resemble mortuary filing cabinets. You rent a minimal drawer for the night and there you sleep on a futon, for the futon is minimalist bedding.

It is the bedmaker's dream and the sleeper's nightmare. It is the mattress you have when you're not having a mattress, and yet when the futon was chic the makers could charge what they wished. It was an expensive way of sleeping on the floor. Like *nouvelle cuisine* the futon is a con, and like *nouvelle cuisine* it has died. From its ashes has risen the Scandinavian slat-bed.

In unappealing Castle Lindo in Leicestershire I saw a bed that Elizabeth the First is supposed to have slept in. It appeared to have slats across its base, but I realise now that it could not have done, because the slat-bed is as modern as trim-pork.

My neighbour has a Scandinavian slat-bed. She told me what a wonder it is, 'but,' she added, 'you have to have a really good mattress.' I asked why. She looked at me as if I were dandruff. 'So you can't feel the slats,' she said.

Slats will fall, of course, and something will rise in their stead. We, the buyers of beds, have three options: we can mock fashion, follow it or lead it. I have decided to lead it.

I am about to patent a sort of net slung between poles. I shall call it 'le hammock'. It's cheap to make and seriously uncomfortable. It should go down a treat in the nicer suburbs.

Be the boss

Don't give in to technology. Stand up to it and beat it. Never forget that it is the slave and you are the master.

My bedroom light fizzled then died. I padded to the cupboard to fetch a replacement bulb.

One week and three trips to the supermarket later, I remembered to buy one. The dead bulb had held sixty watts, so I bought one containing a hundred. It should last almost twice as long.

I stood on the bed. Mine is a dead bed. It has sagged into the shape of a rowing boat. I straddled it, balancing on its gunwales with the ease of a trawlerman in a gale. I reached up for the light-bulb.

Raising both hands above one's head does little for the balance. It is why trawlers don't have electric lights. Nevertheless I removed the light bulb. I did this by not letting go of it as I fell. The glass came away nicely in lots of little pieces. Some of them even had blood on them, making a decorative effect on my snowy bachelor bed linen.

Close technical inspection revealed that I had indeed removed the bulb. What I hadn't removed is what home handymen call the metal thing that fits into the thing. I headed for the toolbox for pliers.

One week and three trips to the supermarket later, I remembered to buy a pair of pliers. They were made in Taiwan with green plastic handles and they cost agreeably little. They were of a variety called 'Heavy Duty'.

I played trawlerman again. The thing that was stuck in the thing came out with a sharp crack. A chunk of the thing it was stuck into broke off. The pliers broke too. Undaunted I inserted the new bulb. It lit up.

A hand full of working electricity unnerves me. I leapt down into the rowing boat, deftly catching the bulb as it fell. I turned the light switch to off, climbed back up on deck, slid the bulb in again and twisted it into place. It fell out. Peering into the thing I saw that the bit of the thing I had broken off was the bit of the thing that held the thing on the light bulb in place. It wasn't just a light bulb I needed. I needed an entire new thing.

One week and three trips to the supermarket later, I remembered to find out that the supermarket doesn't sell things. I needed to go to a specialist thingmongers. I thought of getting a man in, but pride said no. The wallet agreed.

The man in the electrical bits shop smiled when I explained in technical terms exactly what I was looking for. It was the smile of one expert to another, a sort of electrical freemasonry. In no time at all he unearthed exactly the right thing. 'That's exactly the right thing,' I said. He smiled again and both the other assistants smiled too. I liked the electrical bits shop.

Electrical repairs require one big decision. If you don't turn off the mains you risk death by electrocution. If you do turn off the mains you have to reset the clock on the microwave. And on the video, and on the oven and on the bedside table. I always choose death by electrocution. Apparently it's swift and you get to look like Rod Stewart.

Pausing only to write my will, I fetched a screwdriver from the toolbox.

One week, three trips to the supermarket and one to Placemakers later, I had acquired a gift pack of fifteen screwdrivers with blue plastic handles. They were made in Taiwan. I was ready.

Our physics teacher was called Glegg. Glegg was strange. He told us that electricity consisted of a chap called Mr Volt standing in a box. Mr Volt spent his life pushing barrels out of the box and round a circuit. The barrels were called amps. I bore this in mind as I applied my screwdriver to the things that attached the wires to the thing. In the style of all good electricians I also screwed my eyes up and stopped breathing.

Glegg also taught us that there were three wires. One was the live wire, one was the earth wire and the other wire was another wire. They came in different colours. I couldn't remember the colours.

It didn't matter. There were only two wires attached to the thing. Both were black. Electricity has obviously changed.

When I detached the broken thing the light shade fell off with it. I put it aside and attached the new thing to the wire. It was easy. I inserted the light bulb. It stayed inserted. Dismounting the trawler deck I started breathing again and turned the switch. The light went on. I tried not to smile. I failed badly. I wished I had Glegg's phone number. I went to put the light shade back. I found that to put the light shade back I needed to detach the new thing. I put the light shade on the floor and went to bed. Masterfully.

The birds and the bees

How lovely to see sex education back in the forum of public debate. I can think of no other topic that offers more scope for sounding off to absolutely no effect.

Sex and education come from different planets. Sex attracts children; education repels them. Bringing the two together is like mating a panther with a wart-hog.

Nevertheless, some people make a career out of telling children about sex. Such people come in two species. Those of the first species have severe mouths, spectacles and haircuts. They wield words like 'morality' which children find deeply moving. Those of the second species wield guitars. They smile a lot, congratulate themselves on their frankness, and sing songs with titles like 'I'm a merry condom'.

Both groups have a profound effect on adults; they induce horror and nausea, respectively. Neither has the least effect on children.

My sexual education counsellor was Dave Parmenter. Dave had Prince Charles ears, oddly shaped knees, and a knowledge of matters sexual that few eight-year-olds could rival.

Dave's sex lecture was thrilling and anatomically bang-on. He didn't say much about alternative life-style choices but he drew superb diagrams in the mud with a stick. I listened rapt and believed none of it. It was all too bizarre to be possible, so I sought out that wellspring of wisdom, Miss Turner, a turkey-throated 630-year-old spinster who taught us English and singing. When she sang her throat wobbled.

When I told Miss Turner what Dave Parmenter had told me, I don't think she believed it either. Briefly, and uniquely, I saw her throat tighten. It was only a glimpse, however. Once I had spat the soap out of my mouth Miss Turner told me to watch the birds and the bees.

So I did. I watched thousands of meaningful inter-avian encounters without learning much. The male leaps on the female amid a flurry of feathers, pecks her on the neck a couple of times and then flies back to the pub. If the earth moves, it does so with haste. Obviously thousands of men have taken the bird-lesson to heart.

The trouble with the birds, however, is that it's not at all clear what's going on where it matters. One can understand why bird-watching becomes a life-long hobby and needs a zoom lens.

As educators, bees were even worse. I followed bees around for weeks without ever seeing any of them engage in meaningful inter-apian rumpety-pumpety. I have since been told that they sport in the privacy of the hive and the business involves hundreds of males crawling over one fat female. Did Miss Turner know that?

There is nothing new under the sun. The same debate as is raging now was raging thirty years ago. As John Mortimer observed at the time, the young had suddenly discovered in the swinging 1960s that it was possible and fun to go to bed together. But, he added, they made the same discovery in the swinging 1410s.

The attitude

So now at last it is time to present the main award of the evening, the Mrs Ritchie-Hook Cup for lying.

A woman of substance sits on the handlebar of a bicycle while her less substantial fancy boy pedals her through an orchard. Off camera a band plays mush. Meanwhile someone has smeared the camera-lens with gold-tinted vaseline.

Propelling the lassie up a hill proves beyond fancy boy's strength. They wobble, they totter, then they tumble off the bicycle into a wood pile. If either of them had any sense they would then lie down to play doctors and nurses.

But no. Fancy boy spies a chainsaw, and being a fancy boy of resource, sexual inadequacy and a degree in automotive engineering he attaches the chainsaw to the bicycle. They remount, as it were. The bicycle buzzes nicely up the hill. The final shot is a silhouette of the buxom one spreading her legs in joy. Or sexual invitation. Or a bid to save her ankles from the chainsaw.

Apparently, this little story demonstrates 'the attitude'. The advertiser is trying to suggest that 'the attitude' is the undaunted attitude. Don't worry if you fall off. Use your ingenuity, be a good fix-it chappie and your reward will come in the form of a large girl on a bicycle. Your sexual success will also be supported by an invisible band and a camera crew.

Now, to demonstrate that we too have 'the attitude' we have to buy lottery tickets. They are called scratch-and-win tickets. That's a lie for a start. They are scratch-and-lose tickets. If they weren't there wouldn't be a lottery.

But the bigger lie, the real whopper, the fib at the heart of a sad civilisation lurks in the advertisement.

Buying a lottery ticket in the remote hope of winning a lot of lolly is an all too human activity. In other words, it is lazy and feeble and greedy and stupid. The ad, however, suggests that buying a lottery ticket is an ingenious solution to the problems of life. That's a fib. A deliberate porky-pie.

But yes, of course, I know, I do so agree, it's just a silly ad on the telly; it doesn't matter.

But it does matter; it matters a lot. It matters because in this ad the image and the truth have got divorced. And in the divorce settlement the image got all the cash.

If we snuggle up to the image and spurn the truth then we are in trouble. The ground falls away beneath our feet. We are left spinning in a void where nothing means anything. We become susceptible to all sorts of nonsense.

Already we have the Steinlager All Blacks and the DB Bitter Warriors. Does nobody mind that beer makes us fat, incoherent and liable to fall over? If the All Blacks drank a lot of beer they would lose. Maybe the Warriors do. And does it matter that most of the Canterbury Crusaders don't come from Canterbury? And what are they crusading for? And how can the brewery call it 'our beer'? It isn't our beer; it's their beer. They're trying to sell it to us. And do we believe that 'everyone gets a bargain'? I don't get a bargain. I get something that breaks.

'But,' squeak the darlings, 'this is the 1990s. This is commercial reality.' It may or may not be the 1990s, but it is definitely not reality. It's illusion.

Advertising is famous for its nonsense. But if we are not careful it won't stop there. If we continue to confuse image and substance we will suffer. I am willing to bet a pound of pumpkins to a pod of peas that the time will come when we are so dazzled by image and so negligent of truth that we will elect to the second highest political office in the land a proven charlatan. Mark my words.

Nevertheless, I believe the creative sweeties who made the lottery ads won an award. I'd like to give them another one. And here to present it is Mrs Ritchie-Hook herself.

Bomb the bastard

Bomb the bastard. Don't hesitate, devastate. Blast him, shoot him, crucify and nuke him, for I need entertaining.

Call off that Madeleine Albright. When you're talking war you don't send in your granny with the soft fat arms. Besides, there's never any point in bandying words with a bloke with a moustache who wears battle-dress in bed. Dust off Stormin' Norman and let's get cracking.

It's been seven long years with nothing decent on telly. I need a war. Remember those smart bombs that could turn left at traffic lights? Only problem in the last show was it was all in black and white, but they've had plenty of time to fix that. They've got a bomb now that's so smart you can show it a photograph of the target and it'll go find it. They should show it a mug shot of the chief nutter himself and then let it loose to sniff round the presidential palace, trying the doorhandles, checking the cupboards till it runs the dingbat to earth in one of his presidential lavatories and has him cowering up against his gold-plated jacuzzi showing his teeth and promising to shave his moustache and marry a Jew all relayed on prime-time through NoseCam to a global audience of civilised television-owning democrats which means us and we're all on our feet screaming 'Get the madman' and 'Give him one for me' and then Whammo! it's time to crack open the bubbly. Beats *The Darling Buds of May*, though that Zita something or other, she's a belter.

Great place to have a war. Miles away from anyone who matters. To be sure, the old fruitcake has got eight presidential palaces with more spare bedrooms than you can shake a stick at and every one of them crammed to the ceiling with fifty-seven varieties of bio-logical nasty while his harem has to make do with the servants' quarters, but if you think about it the whole place is surrounded by billions of miles of sand, so give it the Cruise missile treatment, I say. The stuff will all soak away in a year or two, and if a few camels come down with a dose of anthrax, well, frankly, who gives a monkey's? I've never seen the point of camels myself. Sandra went on one of those coach tours of the pyramids and she reckoned there was this one camel would bite you soon as look at you. It had yellow eyes, Sandra said. It used to spit as well. Yellow spit.

That nerve-gas stuff, too, if you think about it, it's all in our favour. One whiff of Sarin and you go all liquid inside and swell up to twice your normal size, and if you fall over you can't get up. So when Uncle Sam dumps the Semtex this stuff gets sprayed all over Baghdad and then when the Marines move in they find the elite Iraqi fighting force rolling around in the dunes like so many Mr Blobbies. Apparently you can finish them off by just popping them with a pin. Great television. I think I'll get Sky. CNN's un-beatable on that sort of stuff.

So what's holding us back? Why aren't the boys out there in the Persian Gulf right this minute chalking skull and crossbones on the bomb-bays of the B52's? Scuds? Don't make me laugh. You don't make a serious missile and call it Scud. Sounds like some-thing left in the bath. Remember when the balloon went up last time all we ever saw of the Scuds was file footage of the things being carted around the desert on trucks having nets thrown over them. They didn't even point up at the sky. And anyway, even if one of them did freakishly get off the ground and start homing in on Tel Aviv, the Yanks would have the whole place surrounded with those brilliant Patriot things that stand bolt upright like proper missiles and cost about three zillion bucks each. One hint of a Scud on the radar and every Patriot in the Middle East would spring to attention and blast the thing out of the sky before you could say Star-Spangled Banner.

Sure, a few civilians are going to cop it, but as my old gran used to say, you can't make an omelette without a casualty or two. And to be honest, it might knock a bit of sense into the rest of them. I feel sorry for them in a way, those Iraqis, I do really. I mean they don't know any better, do they? They've just been fed a whole lot of lies from start to finish, all that business about the will of Allah, and American imperialist dogs, and of course you can't get Sky in Iraq, oh nosirree, every foreign TV signal is intercepted and scrambled at the border so all they get is *Your 101 Best Fig Recipes* and the local six o'clock news written by Saddam's rent boy.

I reckon that if you gave them half an hour of Judy Bailey and a couple of All Black tests live they'd soon storm the presidential palaces themselves and have the divine leader dangling by his testicles from the nearest mosque. That would be okay, I suppose, as long as CNN got there in time.

Animal porn

Like you, whenever I hear the word 'pornography' I immediately think of Africa. And in particular I think of well-I-never, such-wonderful-photography-don't-you-think, and did-you-see-that-one-about-rhinos Sunday evening nature programmes like *Our World*. They're filth.

David Attenborough's up to his nineteenth-century-explorer shorts in guano in the depths of a forest in Borneo or some other equally unspeakable part of Africa and he's smiling because he and his trusty eighteen-man camera crew, chef, twenty-six-wheeled air-conditioned bus, personal trainer and shorts-designer, have finally tracked down the almost-extinct Bornean giant leech. The said leech is at present battling the threat of extinction by sucking as much blood as it can out of David Attenborough's scrawny thigh in the time needed to get a few close-ups of its hideous proboscis, after which the personal trainer hauls the leech off with a sort of schlurpy noise and then stamps on it. If he's got any sense, that is.

But he hasn't got any sense, none of them have, otherwise they'd be sitting at home drinking beer and watching the telly and working for Inland Revenue rather than hotfooting it after leeches.

But what really gets me about nature porn is the way they make animals out to be nice. Animals aren't nice. They're animals.

Somewhere on the plains of the Mekong Delta – don't expect me to be precise; Africa's all one to me – there's a woman in sweaty safari gear and no make-up whispering reverentially into a camera about a pack of cheetahs which she's been following around for three years now, and which treat her as one of the family – the odd one with no visible fur who always sits on top of an armour-plated Landrover with a camera – and to which she has given names.

There's Long Paws (after the play by Harold Pinter – literary in-joke. Ignore it.) and Squat Face and poor little limping Diddums, and the big worry is whether Diddums the infant cheetah is going to be able to murder enough zebra to get him through the next rainy season. We all hold our breath throughout the rainy season which happily coincides with the ad-break.

But all that's actually needed to get weak little Diddums through the rainy season is for the grinning Yes-Massa driver to ram the Landrover into first and power away towards the fleshpots of Nbongo with enough force to dislodge nine stone of little Miss Safari-suit from the roof and leave her squealing and alone under a vast and remorseless African sky to discover how Diddums actually feels about their really rather special relationship. What she will swiftly discover is that Diddums has got the emotional complexity of a kitchen appliance and great big teeth.

That, however, is the stuff of fantasy. Instead we get those magnificently phoney sequences with a snapshot of Diddums looking up and pricking his ears accompanied by a voice-over saying 'but suddenly Diddums catches sight of a movement in the undergrowth' at which point we cut to ancient file footage of a wildebeest. Meanwhile Yes-Massa has been despatched with a shotgun and returns with a sack of wounded wildebeest, which are then let loose at intervals until Diddums finally manages to nail one.

Which of course is why most people watch. They like the killing. The producers are perfectly well aware of this so they do all the slaughter in slo-mo. And it's always the good-guy animals that get to tear hunks out of the still-twitching bellies of the animals that don't look anything like the family pet and which are anyway so stupid and numerous that it doesn't matter if they die.

If you get sucked in by the inch-thick emotional loading of these 'programmes' try giving the wildebeest names. It all seems a bit different when the cheetah is burying its teeth into an oesophagus that belongs to Emma. Better still, call them all brutes and change channels.

Ah yes, but, it's *educational*. Well, that's what they all say, in particular those bulky men in shiny tuxedos who stand outside places in Manchester Street smoking. 'Come on in, son,' they say, 'it's edu-cational.' (Such men have a point of course. Take the invitation and dance up those dimly lit red-carpeted stairs and you can learn a lot of good stuff.)

But you won't learn any good stuff from *Our World* even though it's fronted by the profoundly educational Richard Long. The reason you won't learn any good stuff is that it's all lies.

If you want to learn good stuff about, say, scorpions, get stung by one. That's exactly fifty per cent of everything you need to know about scorpions. The other fifty percent is the best way of killing them.

It's napalm.

The essence of Sunday

When I was young museums were like Sundays – oppressive, depressing and adult. Historically museums have served several purposes within our cultural framework. The first of these has been to provide somewhere for tourists to go when it is raining.

Obviously, however, museums have always served one main purpose and for the well-being of our society they must continue to do so. They hold our yesterdays for the sake of our tomorrows. Traditionally museums have been places to which adults have brought their children in order to teach them their cultural identity by boring them to a coma.

The first essential of boring a child is silence. Churches invented the idea. Libraries took it up. Museums perfected it.

Silence delights middle-class, middle-aged adults. It is the distilled essence of Sunday afternoon. Nothing more thrills the adult soul than to stand in raincoat, sensible shoes and silence before a well-organised display of bird-skeletons.

In a traditional museum one is expected to walk slowly, gawp and say shhhh. Adults like doing these things.

Museums further gratify adults by being educational. Educational in this sense doesn't mean that you learn stuff. It means that you can convince yourself that you are learning stuff. A typical educational activity in this sense of the word is thumbing through *National Geographic* for pictures of naked African women.

The sad truth is that for all their good intentions traditional museums are overwhelming. One marvels at this exhibit or that but learns little. There is simply so much to see, so much to read. Nine visitors out of ten emerge from a museum wondering quite what they went in for. The tenth is found at closing time snoring amid dinosaurs.

Children, of course, don't like to walk, gawp or be silent. They like to run, scream and break things. But because museums are meant to teach, and teaching is something we inflict on children, today's curator seeks to lure the child. His bait is the interactive exhibit.

In the local museum there is a wall of buttons with photographs of birds beside them. Press one of those buttons and reasonably soon you will hear the call of the bird in the photograph. It is a highly educational display. Only today, indeed, I saw a child with hair like a porcupine learn that if you press all the buttons at once you can make a lot of adults scowl at you as you run away.

There is also an artificial cave. Children crawl in one end and emerge from the other end. From this they learn that if you crawl in one end of a cave you will emerge from the other end.

I do not know what lurks inside this cave. I am an adult and so I don't do interactive stuff. I am afraid of looking foolish.

For this reason it was with nervous tread that I visited the Museum of New Zealand, the notorious Te Papa, for Te Papa is the home of interactivity. And how the children flock to it. Indeed one's first thought as one passes through the vast portals of Te Papa is what a lot of flocking children.

Te Papa has banished the oppressive silence of the traditional museum. When not making noise, the children are queueing to get in to the seriously interactive things. It's remarkably similar to a cinema complex. They seem to like it.

For the adult the change from a traditional museum is equally startling since Te Papa denies any gulf between high and low culture. Working on the notion that everything is culture thay have placed a 1960's fridge alongside a 1960's painting by Colin McCahon. I rather liked the fridge.

Te Papa has the world's greatest collection of escalators and lifts. As a learned art critic friend observed, one immediately gets that department store feeling; and with a skill one can only admire, the good folk of Te Papa have recreated exactly that talent of department store escalators and lifts for carrying you past somewhere you wanted to go to somewhere you didn't want to go and can't quite find your way out of.

Te Papa is the museum of New Zealand. They have sought to capture the essence of the nation, to hold a mirror up for us to see ourselves. In a curious sort of way they have succeeded.

Gone is that austere oppressive reverence that one associates with colonial New Zealand, traditional museums and church. What has replaced it is the spirit of that modern place of worship, the shopping mall. Like a shopping mall it is full of kids and lights and a few things you like and lots of things you can't see the point of. Te Papa has a sense of energetic chaos.

It is glitzy, eclectic and unrefined. I don't think any more learning goes on there than it does in traditional museums, and though no doubt its intentions are scholarly, its mood is popular.

What Te Papa has done is to shift the idea of a museum in this country from age to youth, from seriousness to levity and, most importantly, from Sunday to Saturday. I rather like it.

Words words words

'I am sorry to have written you such a long letter,' wrote Pascal in 1656, 'but I didn't have time to write a short one.' If only the people in charge of education had studied Pascal at school.

In her weighty article defining the role of the Educational Review Office, spokesperson Judith Aitken says very little in a lot of words. In doing so she is maintaining the best traditions of the overlords of education in New Zealand, the waffle-mongers of the New Zealand Qualifications Authority (NZQA).

To take a paragraph almost at random from Dr Aitken's article, *'If we have reason to be concerned about the way the national curriculum is taught in a particular school, our judgment of that school's professional teaching services to its own students will be shaped by that finding.'* If this were a student's essay I would first cross out the words *particular, professional* and *services to its own students* and ask if anything had been lost. Then I would put a squiggly line in the margin and ask what the whole paragraph actually means. I presume it means that if the Education Review Office finds bad teaching it will say so. I hope it does mean that because that is the Education Review Office's job.

The rest of the article says much the same thing. It just takes about a thousand words to say it.

Does it matter that Dr Aitken writes marshmallow English? In some fields it might not, but in education it does. Teachers are in the business of encouraging clarity of thought. Most rational thinking is done through words. Muddy words betray muddled thinking.

On my classroom wall is a lovely thing called a Buzzword Generator. It consists of three columns of words. By taking a word at random from each column one creates delicious phrases like 'monitored delivery system' and 'integrated asssessment context'. Clearly Dr Aitken has a Buzzword Generator. She also kindly lent it to the NZQA to help them write the new curriculum for the subject of English.

The language in which much of this curriculum is written leaves one gasping. Many phrases of apparent importance are meaningless. What are *'listening behaviours'* or *'information skills'* or *'language events'* or *'authentic contexts'*? This is no petty point. There's a grisly irony in a document that purports to be a blueprint for the teaching of English throughout the country but which uses the language so badly. Am I supposed to take *'focused inter-personal listening skills'* seriously?

From the lovely new curriculum have sprung the lovely Unit Standards. These outline the skills that students learn as they get taught. Each time they jump one of these hurdles they get credit. Unit Standards are supposed eventually to replace exams.

The idea of Unit Standards has some merit. We all know how unfair exams are, although I have to say that in twenty years of teaching I have noticed that those students who deserve to do well in exams tend to do so and those who don't, don't. Nevertheless the premise of Unit Standards, that we recognise what students can do and reward them for that, is laudable.

If the draft Unit Standards in English stated clearly and emphatically what a student had to do to pass them, they could work. But they don't. They are unwieldy, unworkable and silly. Their faults spring from woolly thinking which in turn springs from woolly language.

As an example, the draft Unit Standard for English *E1.8 Oral Language: Personal Reading Level 1* states that *People credited with this unit standard are able to: select an inclusive range of oral texts; 'read' selected texts; and maintain a record of the 'reading' experience.* Isn't that nice? But what does it mean?

Readers may be interested to learn that an 'oral text' means a bit of spoken language that has been recorded, such as a radio programme or a speech. These 'texts' must *demonstrate gender inclusiveness.* So presumably the first skill that students must master is choosing some recordings of both men and women. Tricky stuff.

Then they've got to 'read' them. 'Read' doesn't mean read. 'Read' means 'listen to and think about'. This of course is hijacking the language and delightfully reminiscent of Humpty Dumpty in *Alice Through the Looking Glass* who insisted that words meant what he wanted them to mean.

Unit Standards won't work. I do not need to shoot them down here; they will topple of their own accord. There are numerous reasons why they will topple, but one of them is the language in which they are written. When the word 'read' doesn't mean read, nor 'text' text, nor 'poetic' poetic, then we have entered a world where meaning itself dissolves. Indeed, the word 'unit' means nothing and 'standards' under the proposed system will be anything but standard.

We live in a world ruled by language. Dr Aitken, the NZQA and all our children should all read George Orwell's *Politics and the English Language*. From it they would learn that good language is a scalpel and that bad language is a smokescreen. Words have meanings. To desert those meanings is naughty. If Dr Aitken, the NZQA and all our children remain unconvinced, let them interview a man whose limbs have been severed from his body by friendly fire. Let them ask him what 'friendly' means.

The work of the ERO matters a lot, and Dr Aitken's badly written article does little harm. Nevertheless its inflated language is typical of our educational bureaucracy. At best such language is window-dressing; when it dictates how we teach the young it is actively dangerous.

Pascal may have written 300 years ago but he has much to teach us.

The tongue-thing

So, the lassie has a thing through her tongue. It is a silver thing, a sort of dwarf weightlifter's dumb-bell, and she has developed the charming knack of making one end of it protrude between her lips and then wiggling it from side to side. Thus she has added her bit to the popular art of body-piercing, an art much practised among primitive peoples. Indeed the number of holes in this girl's flesh and the tonnage of silver bangles dangling from them may well denote high rank, but today I am concerned only with the dumb-bell through the tongue.

And I am not alone in being concerned with the dumb-belled tongue. The nasty principal of this girl's high school is also concerned with it, so very concerned that he has told her to remove it. She refused. He suspended her from school.

Enter the lassie's father, frothing with indignation as protective fathers of vulnerable children understandably tend to do. And, of course, he sat her down, told her in forthright terms to remove the dumb-bell, apologised to the principal and sent the lassie to bed without any supper.

Or so we would have supposed. But we would have supposed wrong. Instead, dear papa gave her a pat on the back and a tube of Brasso for the dumb-bell and then informed the fascist principal that his daughter would remove the dumb-bell only over dad's dead body, and while he was still breathing she would continue to attend school.

The nub of dad's argument was that the school had contravened an inalienable human right, the right to freedom of expression. His daughter wanted to wear the tongue-thing; the tongue-thing was, indeed, a profound expression of who she was, and the bossy little schoolmaster had no right to crush her individuality.

Well, now, it has been a hot summer. Let us suppose the daughter had chosen to attend school naked (except of course for the tongue-thing, which I would imagine is pleasantly cool in the mouth when the wind is from the nor-west). Would dear papa have let her? Would he have crushed her free spirit?

Or were she to decide to go to live with baboons in whatever ghastly country baboons live in, or to become pregnant, or to insist on eating only cat-biscuits, would papa nod his head, smile, pat her on the back and say, 'that's my girl'? He would? Then he is nuts.

No doubt dad would argue that his daughter is doing nobody any harm by piercing and embellishing her tongue. Ignoring the possibility that she may not be doing her tongue a fat lot of good, on the face of things he would seem to be right.

But how faces lie. Let us consider the tongue-thing from the point of view of the school's principal. If he allows the father's argument and admits the right to the tongue thing he will be in no position to reprimand any child who breaks any convention. Freedom of self-expression will be the catch-cry, and soon the principal will find himself in charge of a school where anything goes. Or rather he won't be in charge of it at all.

The result of that is easy to imagine. Parents will remove their children. The school will shrink and then sink and leave not a wrack behind.

We hear an awful lot about rights. Father insists on his daughter's right to express herself. At the same time he implicitly assumes her right to an education. Both rights are indeed enshrined in law in New Zealand. Neither is a natural right. Both are artificially created by an artificially organised society. They are not so much rights as privileges.

If dad is unconvinced by this distinction I invite him to send his daughter to North Korea having first taught her a few choice phrases of self-expression about the president of that country. The authorities would certainly remove his daughter's tongue-thing. Whether they would bother to extract it from her tongue first is less certain.

Or let him send her to Eritrea to insist on her inalienable right to eleven years of education at the state's expense. They love a good laugh in Eritrea.

The rights that this gentleman is insisting on are rare in this world. Most people do not have either of them. They are to be cherished, and should not be invoked for the sake of an infantile whim. *De minimis non curat lex*, which translates loosely as 'stop whining about tongue-pieces, darling, and thank your lucky stars you live in a wealthy democracy.'

And then finally there is the question of age. Father insists that his daughter knows best. At what age did she start knowing best? At fifteen, or ten, or five? Or was she pretty clued-up in the womb? And if she knows best, if she is capable of making adult decisions for herself, then what need has she for school? School is a place of training. His daughter does not apparently need any form of training. Whatever she does is right.

I have just discovered that one may not become president of the United States until one is 35 years old. The hoary old birds who knocked up the Constitution clearly thought that if you have lived that long you have enough experience to talk sense. How wrong they were. Witness several presidents and one New Zealand father.

The late and the punctual

G.K. Chesterton said that the only way he knew to catch a train was to miss the one before. I admire Chesterton's ability to be late for everything, to be so busy and happy and alive that he could discount time.

'Punctuality is a courtesy,' I tell the children who arrive late for class. They protest that they didn't hear the bell or were too engrossed in Physics or had to foil a bank-robbery. If they lie badly I punish them. If they lie creatively I laugh, congratulate them and punish them. Both of us know it's a ritual. They will be late again tomorrow. The same children. They're late people.

And oddly the late people often sparkle. They're the different ones, the challengers and arguers. Late people smile more than punctual people.

I have heard it said that punctual people have never snapped their mothers' apron strings. The punctual feel the constant need to please, to placate, to earn praise. They define themselves by what other people think of them. Late people, on the other hand, are on the other hand. They do not care what others think. They have been weaned from the milk of praise.

Punctual people tend to be nicer than late people. They're also more boring. I have taught hundreds of earnest, decent, punctual children. I have forgotten most of them. But I shall never forget Rolf Wilkinson. Rolf defined lateness.

I taught Rolf in the early eighties but his manner was pure flowers-in-your-hair Woodstock. Even his life was a decade late. Rolf's head manufactured its own hallucinogens. He spoke exactly like Dylan in *The Magic Roundabout*.

On the wing for my under-15C rugby team Rolf played a roving role. He often roved into a different game.

One Friday Rolf came to me, his brows knitted like a scarf. 'Hey, like, sir, like I don't think I can like play whatsit tomorrow,' he said lucidly, 'It's sorta like, me mum, she's like going away.'

After questioning Rolf for well under an hour I gathered that he couldn't play rugby because his mother would not be able to drive him to the game. When I suggested to Rolf that he could catch a bus to school he looked at me as if I'd spoken Hebrew. But with the help of a kindly telephone we discovered that a Number 6 bus stopped outside Rolf's house and would deliver him in time for an eleven o'clock kick-off. I wrote '6' on a piece of paper to help him.

Saturday morning. Eleven o'clock came and Rolf didn't. We played with 14 and lost narrowly. Had Rolf turned up we would have lost more comfortably.

Nevertheless, on the Monday morning I cornered Rolf, intending to give him a piece of my mind. The piece I was thinking of stinks like a trawler and contains several of the words I learned from the lovely man who used to hang around the kindergarten.

'So what's the story, Rolf?' I began mildly.

Rolf gave me his puzzled-Hebrew-interpreter look again.

'Saturday,' I said, 'the rugby. You were going to catch a bus.'

In the psychedelic chaos of Rolf's mind, the sun rose. He beamed. 'Hey, like, yeah, the bus. Man, that bus, it went some like weird places.' At this point Rolf wandered off into dreamland, revisiting the memories of his journey. He smiled beatifically.

It turned out that Rolf had indeed caught a Number 6 bus. He had caught it at the right time and the right place. How was he to have known that this Number 6 bus was going in the wrong direction?

I gave Rolf a detention after school. Four o'clock arrived and Rolf didn't.

Waffle Revisited

In a recent article I sniped at waffle. I described pompous language, particularly the language of educational theory, as a smokescreen. It was pretty mild sniping, but the reaction staggered me. I have received a stream of letters from teachers, nurses, lawyers, doctors, university professors and men and women from the suburban omnibus, almost all of whom wanted to join a crusade against the waffle-mongers. All their professions, it seems, are being choked with words.

A letter from a nurse particularly affected me. She had nursed for years and was obviously good at it. But she said that now she felt stupid. She felt stupid because she couldn't understand the things that were being written about how to be a nurse.

But other letters came too, letters from the wordy ones. A letter from Dr Blackmur, an important chap at the New Zealand Qualifications Authority, particularly delighted me.

You see, as a teacher, I have written to Dr Blackmur's organisation twice and have experienced a zero reply situation, thus restricting my capacity for productive learning outcomes. One newspaper article, however, and hey presto Mr Blackmur and I are engaged in a profitable ongoing dialogue context.

Sadly, however, it isn't dialogue. I wrote about the misuse of language. Mr Blackmur corrected a couple of errors of fact, for which I thank him, and then implied that I was rude and inarticulate. I thank him for that too.

But he said nothing about the charge of inflated language, which was the nub of the article. He is wise not to do so, because to strip away its language might be to strip away NZQA's power.

Holders of power wear words in the same way as royalty wears clothes. Put the Queen in a pair of jeans and we see her differently.

Put the NZQA in its linguistic swimming togs and the public might just start kicking sand in its face.

To put things simply, people in power like to stay in power. One way to stay in power, of course, is to kill people. This can work for a long time. In the end the President Mobutus and the Idi Amins get caught out, but not before they've had a long time having grapes peeled for them.

Killing people is risky, but there is another way to maintain power. This is to make it seem that you are the only person who can do a job. If you use language that people can't understand, then the people tend to presume that you are doing something difficult and impressive. They feel they cannot argue with you.

To take a simple example, let us consider the strategic plan. All self-respecting organisations these days have a strategic plan, and what a jolly nice thing it is. I bet NZQA's got a beauty.

Strategic plans sound weighty and significant. But the dictionary defines 'stratagem' as a plan. So a strategic plan means a planny sort of plan. Now it carries less thump. If they called it a planny sort of plan, then you and I would feel better qualified to contribute to it.

But strategic plans are hard to write. What we need is a consultant to help us write it. Or perhaps a facilitator. Or maybe, and even more expensively, a strategic facilitator hired on a consultancy and implementation basis.

Consultancy, with its aura of medical expertise, is one of today's buzzwords. Consultants hover around the public coffers like flies around dung. Note how many of the current brouhahas about corruption in parliament and the public services involve 'legitimate consultancy fees'.

I know a management consultant. He doesn't, I'm pleased to say, have access to this newspaper. Nor do I have access to his bank account, but I do know that he races motor cars for a hobby, and that I once got lost in his house.

This management consultant has a brief but impressive management record. He set up one small company which fell over within months. At that point his partner ran off with what was

44

left of the cashbox. So he was broke – but he was wise and he could see which way the geese were flying. He became a management consultant. Businesses now pay vast sums for his services.

Private businesses are, of course, welcome to spend their private money on whatever they like. Public services, however, are not, because their money is our money. Nevertheless there is ample evidence that your money and my money is paid to people to spin words that mean nothing.

The Ministry of Education, for example, hires people on contract to assist in 'professional development'. I have in front of me 'the final milestone report' of one such person on the work that he and his team did.

Ironically the field of English teaching that he worked on was entitled 'Exploring Language'. As the whole caboodle was funded by public money, I think we are entitled to read the report and explore its language a little.

'Effective professional development only takes place over time. It needs to be monitored, coordinated and overseen by the Ministry of Education.'

That paragraph is one of his clearer ones in the report but it still shows the classic techniques of the waffler: he uses strings of latinate words to make the obvious sound impressive; he uses three long verbs where one short one would do; he uses the passive voice.

Elsewhere we find, 'If mainly integrated and holistic approaches are taken, then the quality of the knowledge, understanding and skills vital to effective practice and use of the three processes may be insufficient to enable teachers and students to achieve the functions successfully.'

This is thistledown language. At the heart of it lies a tiny seed of something the author has to say, but it is surrounded by such a tissue of fluffy stuff that the seed is invisible. Note the length of the sentence and the words. Note that all the nouns are abstract so there is nothing for the mind to grasp. Note the needless repetition: what is the difference between 'integrated' and 'holistic', or between 'practice' and 'use'? And how on earth does one achieve a function?

'The approach of the programme presenters to training trainers was that coordinators and facilitators already had the necessary generic facilitating skills and that they needed to process and adapt the information, understanding and classroom suggestions from the programme for their clients and their own particular English professional development work.'

Language should communicate. When it doesn't, it is bad language. What is sad is that bad language like this impresses some people and daunts others.

Waffle's a doddle to write. For example, one could easily say that it is a commonly observed phenomenon of contemporary linguistic behaviours that the utilisation of polysyllabic vocables of abstract or indeterminate significance but not inconsiderable production volume is a feature of containers, repositories and receptacles in a condition approaching, and on occasion embracing, voidness.

Or else one could say that empty vessels make most noise.

House hunting

I am seeking a new house. All I have found so far is a new language. I have learned that sad little houses respond to TLC. I was glad to learn that you could make a house happy by hugging it. I had thought houses to be like lovers: hugs are all well and good but in the end they require a lot of money.

I have also learned about society. My mother sheltered me from riff-raff so I have never knowingly met an executive, but from the real estate columns I have discovered that executives don't live in houses. They live in residences. Residences cost several zeros more than houses, but they do have indoor/outdoor living. This is much better than having a garden.

Almost every building for sale that is not a residence is a wee gem. Villas ooze character, space and grace. Summerhill stone is definitely not a drive-by. Wherever I choose to inspect, viewing will impress.

Last weekend an ad for a cottage leapt from the page. I swatted it down and read it. The cottage nestled, apparently, in a secluded easy-care section. I saw hollyhocks and rambling roses, a woman in tweeds with a trug, quaint little dormer windows and, lying on the sun-drenched veranda, a fat tortoiseshell cat for the dogs to dismember. My cottage. I decided to view and be impressed.

As the dogs drove I lounged in the back seat of the turbo mega-butch, permanent-4-wheel-drive, I'm-a-real-tough-cookie, all-terrain recreational vehicle, the sort of vehicle that growing numbers of all-terrain recreational women drive to the shopping mall. The treble overhead cam purred overhead like a tortoiseshell cat. With the dogs singing merry motoring songs I dreamed of my cottage life to come.

I had expected to be able to see my cottage from the road, but I hadn't expected to be able to smell it.

It smelt like the West Coast in the rotting season.

Shielding my eyes from the real-estate agent's grin, I emerged from the car. The real-estate agent pumped my hand, stroked the dogs, introduced himself as Something Hook Norton and handed me his card. I found I had erred. This was no real-estate agent. This was a real-estate consultant. I would have told him how honoured I felt had I been able to take the handkerchief from my nose.

The easy-care section was indeed easy-care. Ten square yards of concrete give little trouble. Fool that I am I had thought that cottages were built of weatherboard or gingerbread. This one was built of fibro-board and flimsy flat stuff. These are permanent materials. The windows were not dormer; they were broken. The exterior was painted a cheerful excrement brown.

The interior, however, was not so attractive. It was built for dwarves with no sense of smell. There clearly had been a tortoiseshell cat, but someone else's dogs had got to it months ago and stashed the remains beneath the floorboards. Shortly afterwards its owner had joined it.

'What a wee gem,' said Consultant Hook Norton, 'a bit of TLC and she'll be good as.'

Therapy

Therapy is in. Therapy is good. The Yanks got it first, but when the Yanks start scratching we all end up with psoriasis.

Just like you I want to go to a trim, mature, sympathetic woman in sharply cut clothes and just a hint of a middle-European accent, and I want to lie down on her couch and I want to burst into tears. 'Help me,' I weep. 'I am small and feeble and middle-class and pink. Help me.'

She says nothing.

I let rip. All my heavy stressed back-of-the-skull weight, I let it explode in her consulting rooms; I burst like a zit. Self-pity drips onto her neutral pastel carpet. The yellowness of my spine irradiates her neutral pastel walls.

She says nothing.

'For God's sake,' I scream, 'can't you see, it's all gone wrong. Therapist, mother, therapist-mother, mend my aching head, my fear, my crippled feelings, my dishonesty. Shake from me this dread. Let me step forth into tomorrow, bold and resolute and honest. Let me tell the man at the top that he should not be at the top. Let me tell the beautiful that they are beautiful. Let me hug children and laugh and sing at outdoor tables in the shade where the food is long and good and Mediterranean and fresh and where we sleep in the afternoon and wake easy. Teach me to live, earth-mother, let me be.'

Half an hour of this blubber and I feel just dandy. I bounce from the couch. I seize her cool hand. Then on impulse I hug her, feeling the little nobbles of her spine and the flattening of her breasts. I slightly dislodge her spectacles. She gives me a warm understanding smile. But she says nothing.

At a desk outside sits a young woman with a stop-watch and a calculator and a box of tissues. She presses the stop-watch. 'Thirty-three minutes today, Mr Bennett, at $7.50 is, let's call it $250.'

'Let's call it $300,' I sing, handing her crispies from the Cashflow machine and snatching a tissue to give me sustenance for the windy street beyond. We part in smiles, she with the dollars and I with a pump in the heart and a mind as easy as thistledown.

It's called therapy. Anyone can do it. I've got a business plan. I'm going to start a therapy chain.

First I'm going to a party. I shall seek out the sad, the ones clutching a drink in both hands and taking an interest in the bookshelves. I sidle over, my sympathetic look worn like a badge, my eyebrows lowered at the sides and raised in the middle. Like a mournful, wondering labrador.

'Have we met?' asks the sad one, suddenly nervous.

I maintain my silence, my enquiring, sympathetic mournfulness.

'It's just…' the sad one begins, 'it's just I don't know anyone here, you see, and I don't seem to be very good at mixing, you know. It's always been like that. My mother used to say…' and they're away. I stand, I lean, I listen. I nod and I cluck and I listen.

When the tears start I press my business card into the damp hand, pat the wrist in reassurance and say, 'Just give my secretary a ring.'

From there it snowballs. The sad men and the sad women come and talk to me and feel better and pay me and tell their friends. And I never say a word.

Then I branch out. I make lifesize replica balloon me's and I plant them beside couches in offices in Los Angeles and Sydney. Balloon me's in Ulan Bator and Tashkent. I charge by the minute. $7.50 a minute to strip the emotional clothes in front of a balloon with labrador eyebrows. The MacDonald's of therapy. We'll all be happier.

I'll be so rich I'll need therapy. I'll go to myself.

How to be famous

A ndy Warhol painted soup cans. This made him famous. But Mr Warhol was of a generous disposition. He reckoned that in the future everyone would be famous for fifteen minutes.

Fame is seductive stuff, and though the paths of glory lead but to the grave, many of us still yearn for a posse of paparazzi, even if it is for just a quarter of an hour.

A glance at God's filofax might reveal, however, that you're booked in for your quarter of an hour at 4am on a Sunday, in which case you must take fate into your own hands.

The first step to fame is to get onto television news. An increasingly popular way of doing so is to acquire an Uzi and do target practice in public and on it. It doesn't matter where in the world you do this; the cameras will come to you. So, unfortunately, will the law.

A safer route to stardom is to arrange for a member of your family to die in spectacular fashion. The cameras will sniff you out as a grief-stricken relative, at which point you must be ready. You need a photograph album, the pages of which you must turn mournfully. Sobbing's a bonus, and so is a floral sofa, but never forget that in television terms grief means a photo album.

A slower but less drastic method of hitting the six o'clock screen is to dress up as a scientist. Television news works on the theory that no one can understand a technical item without pictures of a scientist doing something with test-tubes. What you do with the test-tubes is immaterial; it just has to look sciency. The investment – a white coat, inch-thick glasses, two dozen test-tubes, false beard (optional, but worth the effort, especially for women) and an Einstein wig – is nugatory. If you strike it lucky you could become file footage.

There's also a niche for those with theatrical gifts. Dress as a pantomime cow and slither around on wet concrete. If you manage a truly spongiform performance you might replace the clip of the stumbling heifer that accompanies any reference to Mad Cow Disease.

At greater cost but with absolute certainty of televisual success, go to Bangladesh and wait for a disaster. You won't have to wait long. Within days a flood, typhoon or train-crash will wipe out a sizeable tonnage of local citizens. Hasten to the scene and just wait to be discovered. If you want top billing, smear yourself with blood from the carnage and put your arm in a sling. Working on the formula that one lightly bruised Kiwi has the news value of four thousand dead Bangladeshis you'll be a star. But do warn your relatives. The cameras back home will find them. They must have photo albums handy.

For the less adventurous the easiest way to the screen is through an animal. Take one dog and train it to befriend a pig, or else get your vet to make it cross-eyed – a simple and relatively inexpensive procedure, and he might throw in lop-sided ears for the same price. If you can then teach the mutt to howl in time to the Bee Gees, so much the better. The slot you're aiming for is the ooh-aaah bit after the weather, so cuteness is essential, sentiment every-thing. If your dog ain't cute, kill it. There's plenty more at the pound.

Your last resort is the weather itself. Don't imagine you have to know anything about anticyclones, depressions and isobars. The weather report is mainly devoted to telling us what weather we have just had. You will have to learn, however, to pronounce the names of towns in a way that none of the locals do, and you will need a wardrobeful of wacky ties and a fund of folksy humour.

If all this fails and you still want fame, try painting groceries.

Cars and frying pans

Cars are like frying pans. The key to both is to do nothing to them.

All food can and should be fried. The best frying pans are those big black French jobs that strain your wrists. In the hands of a trained chef they can kill burglars.

If you let a such a pan mature, and in particular if you let a decent depth of fat develop in it, it will fry anything. If after several months the fat becomes so deep that you lose sausages in it, then the solution is to eat takeaways for a couple of days while the fat solidifies. It can then be turned out onto a plate and cut into squares. Crunchy Cholesterol Slice is its proper title, and it is best buttered.

The fatal error with frying pans is to wash them. Water affects their chemical composition, making the potassium ions covalent. This means that, after washing, the surface of the pan has thousands of microscopic hands reaching up like those waving sea anemones on coral reefs which are common on television but rare in Lyttelton Harbour.

Crack an egg into a washed pan and all the little hands will clutch onto the electrons in the eggwhite. The egg will stick to the pan like superglue, the only difference being that the bond between the egg and the pan will be strong.

It's much the same with cars. I know quite a lot about cars. I know that red cars go faster than other cars and that men don't drive automatics. I know that driving fast is safer than driving slowly because an accident is a random happening in a random place and so the less time one spends in any random place the less chance one has of meeting the accident lurking there. I also know how to put petrol in, although not how to stop it regurgitating over my shoes, and I know that cars, like frying pans, work better if left alone.

But the society of meddlers have other ideas. Because my big red car is a few years old, the powers of this land, advised no doubt by the brown-suited troglodytes at Occupational Safety and Health, have decreed that every six months when the monster is purring with efficiency it has to be taken to a garage to be mended. This happened to me only two weeks ago. As usual they gave my car a WoF. As usual I gave them just under $1500.

When I got the car back it was immediately evident that they had done an awful lot of work on it. The driver's seat had been adjusted, no doubt to render the mechanic's weekend joyride more comfortable. The mirror had been adjusted too, presumably by the feet of the mechanic's girlfriend.

Further evidence that they had worked long and hard, so to speak, on my car was the fact that it wasn't going as well as when I took it in.

A glance at the docket explained a lot. For a start it explained why mechanics are all young. Having worked for ten years at that hourly rate they retire.

The rest of the docket had all the lucidity of the instruction manual to a Korean VCR. There were words like grommet.

Anyway, true to the frying pan theory, a few days after the car had been fixed, little red warning lamps appeared on the dashboard. I found them quite decorative and ignored them. If you pander to a car's whims it will soon have you opening the bonnet every five minutes.

The car stopped. I turned the key. The engine made the noise of a man flicking through a telephone directory. Then it fell silent.

Now there are two types of car owners. The first type is those who left school early. Such people crawl under stopped cars, adjust the grommets, strip down the carburetor manifold, suck petrol through the sump gasket, spit it out manfully and make the car go.

The other type is the educated few. We are strong on the ontological insecurity of nineteenth-century novelists. When our cars stop we ring the AA as soon as we have finished crying.

My AA man was a charming chap called Chris. He opened the bonnet as if it was the easiest thing in the world, fiddled a bit, then did exactly what I would have done; he fetched a hammer.

At this point I offered to help. After all it was my car and if anyone was going to swing a few blows into the bodywork I had first claim. To my surprise, however, Chris tapped gently at a complicated bit of the engine. To my even greater surprise he didn't make the car start. I think Chris may have stayed on too long at school.

The trouble was the alternator. Obviously. Chris summoned an alternator man who soon told me all I wanted to know about the alternators fitted to Subaru Omegas, which was that they cost $150.

It was dark. I offered to hold a torch for the alternator man. He told me not to bother; he could change an alternator in the dark. And he did.

When I got home I fried some eggs, bread and peas and sat down with a nineteenth-century novel for a good long think.

Stealing the dead

That celebrated thief, an unidentified caucasian male, has strolled into the Auckland Art Gallery, brandished his equally celebrated weapon, a sawn-off shotgun (who does the sawing and why?), torn a painting from the wall, hacked it from its frame, run away and raised all sorts of questions about what is known as the art market.

The painting was by the unfortunately named Tissot, of whom none but the cognoscenti have heard. Tissot's greatest talent, which he shares with all our most valuable artists, is that he is dead. There's nothing like death to boost an artist's reputation. As Van Gogh discovered, self-mutilation is just not enough. You have to go the whole hog and keel over. Half a hog isn't much use, and a mere ear gets you nowhere.

The importance of death in art has been underrated, but the reasons for it are clear enough. It's all to do with economics. Dead painters stop painting. Thus the art market, that bustling throng of bored billionaires, knows for certain how many canvases the corpse has done and can be sure of the value of their investments. They know that if they invest in the dead they will not be faced with the sort of crisis that developed in the phone-card investment industry when a flood of new cards swamped the scene and so sadly turned money to mush.

A further advantage of dead artists is that they can be judged through the spectacles of history. Let us take Monsieur Tissot. Though born in France he inexplicably forsook the huge advantages this gave him with women and moved to England, where he changed his name from the romantic Jacques-Joseph to the rather less romantic James. In England he made a lot of money painting fashionable social occasions. Since then art critics have had a century or so to pin him down, and they have more or less agreed that he lies somewhere in the line of descent from Frith the realist to Whistler the a-bit-less-realist. In short, Tissot's been sussed.

Living artists are harder to suss. Living artists have the vexing habits of changing styles, producing too much and going out of fashion. Not many people understand modern paintings and fewer still like them. Even if they do, they depend on the critics to tell them which ones to like. To buy a modern painting is to gamble. The bored billionaires do not like to gamble. They like to win.

It seems to be agreed by the people who know – though how they know I don't know, and I do sometimes wonder whether they do know or whether they just like to be seen to appear to know on the principle that in the art world the appearance of knowing is more likely than not to be taken for actually knowing because everyone is desperate to know something for sure in this most subjective of subjects – that the unidentified caucasian male stole the Tissot (bless you) to order. The inevitable question is who issued the order.

Are we to believe that somewhere in the States or Switzerland or Saturn there lives a man – it has to be a man, doesn't it? – who is so rich, so lonely and so sad that he yearns to own a painting which he cannot display? Are we to believe that the passion for possession has so filled his soul that he will stoop to this? The answer would appear to be yes.

Is it for the beauty of the thing that the sad one has had it stolen? I somehow doubt it. Is it for its historical significance? I doubt that too. I suspect that, though he may not recognise this truth himself – for how could he live with himself if he did? – he wants to own it because it has an assured financial value and because if he owns it no one else can.

It is a further neat irony that by having it stolen, I guarantee our sad friend has increased its value. It is today a far more celebrated painting than it was last week.

I also bet that the Auckland Art Gallery has had many more visitors through its turnstiles since the theft than it did before. Art with sensation beats art for art's sake.

The urge to make art is fundamental to the human spirit. It is in many ways what makes us human. But there is nothing pure in human affairs. As this ridiculous episode confirms, vanity, greed, pretension and sheer sweet silliness flourish even in the world of art.

In his biography of Dante Gabriel Rossetti, the pre-Raphaelite painter, Evelyn Waugh, the greatest of twentieth-century writers (yes, he's dead), had this to say about some European travels of Rossetti and his pal Holman Hunt:

'They discerned "sweetness" in Fra Angelico, "coarseness" in Rubens, "power" in Leonardo da Vinci and "sympathy for sublime sentiment" in Titian – but no doubt they had a good time.'

I doubt if the same could be said of our sad billionaire.

How you can be as rich as Bill Gates

Bill Gates is nine times as rich as the government of New Zealand. Bill Gates is so rich that he gets to talk to President Clinton. Nevertheless there are advantages to his wealth. For example Bill Gates never wears a tie. Appearing before Clinton less than fully clothed has its dangers, but Gates didn't get where he is today by ducking danger.

The good news, however, is that where Bill Gates had trodden you can tread too. Stick with me and I'll show you how.

But first, let us consider what it means to be that rich. When Bill Gates gets money from the cashflow machine he doesn't check his balance first. Nor, when the cashflow machine is pausing, does he hold his breath. At the Lucky Seven lottery outlet he buys a whole roll of those scratch-and-win tickets and then pays the girl behind the counter to scratch them for him with that dinky little clover-leaf on a chain. Paradise.

In the restaurant Bill Gates has a starter and a main. If he feels like it he has that crayfish dinner for two without worrying if anyone else wants it. He doesn't bring a carrier bag full of warm white wine to a BYO restaurant, and when the bill comes he doesn't get out his calculator and check the menu to find the price of Sharon's crème de cacao which came with a little umbrella but, Sharon said, tasted of petrol. And when he's halfway down the second bottle and just beginning to feel the wind in his conversational sails whereupon the goody-two-shoes waitress minces over and hisses that there's been a complaint from table four and would he mind turning it down a bit, he buys the restaurant and sacks her. Think of being Bill Gates.

On aeroplanes he travels first class which means enough leg-room for a dropsical millipede, seats that go horizontal, no queues for the toilets, prettier stewardesses who do up his safety belt, an overhead locker to himself, *Titanic* rather than *Home Alone 9*, screw-top bottles of French wine, thicker sick bags and getting off first.

And think of Bill Gates's house. He's got an ensuite bathroom and a walk-in wardrobe and a dehumidifier in every room. All his kitchen appliances are by SMEG because of the evocative name and the sexy European styling, and the dishwasher is the same colour as the cupboards so he can pretend he hasn't got one. On the deck there are hundreds of genuine Italian terracotta pots and a barbecue with one of those hood things over it and racks and a rotisserie so that he can cook whole fish perfectly every time as well as the sausages. And when he holds a barbecue he can absolutely fill his garden with those flare things on poles. Heaven.

Bill Gates's car says DOHC on the side and no one dares pronounce it 'dork'. He locks it with one of those beeping remote things which he can programme to play 'Baa Baa Black Sheep'. There's a dodecahedronic stereo with a 350 CD selector in the boot, and it's got 350 CDs in it, and he can open his garage door from anywhere in a twenty-mile radius with a device which turns on the light in the garage at the same time and kills burglars.

And think of being Bill at the supermarket. He just waltzes past the specials and buys huge bleeding hunks of fillet instead of that quick-fry string-vest stuff. And Bill simply heaps his trolley with the very best freeze-dried instant coffee in those fancy jars instead of that powdered own-brand muck which tastes like vacuum-cleaner bags and comes in plastic packets that split when you open them, and even if they do split on him he doesn't have to try and sweep the stuff off the kitchen bench and back into the packet, he just buys a new house and starts filling it with dehumidifiers.

When Bill gets the Innovations catalogue in his morning paper he doesn't have to read it. He orders one of everything. Three days later a parcel arrives with electronic golf-ball washers, an entire home gym and a solar-powered thing for storing shoes. Think of the fun.

Salivating? Want to know how he did it? I'll tell you.

Bill Gates thought positive. He made damned sure at the outset his Attitude was Pointed in the Right Direction. He knew that if he believed it he could do it. He organised himself a Dynamic Thought Pattern and he chose to be the Managing Director of his Own Life. He knew there was no such thing as a dumb idea. He began each day with a Motivational Monologue, did a Super-memory course during his lunch-hours and never went to bed without reciting his Success Inventory. Bill Gates set goals.

He got it all from a little book. It is called *Your Route to Wealth, Health and SMEG,* and is available from all good self-improvement bookshops. Even if it doesn't work for you, think of the purchase as your good deed for the day. Its author is starving.

Biplane or piggybank

Baby animals play games. Baby snakes play sweet little crush-ing-each-other-to-death games and baby lions play let's-rip-throats. The games teach the youngsters to be as vicious as their parents.

Young human beings do the same. The game they play is called Monopoly.

Now I gather that the makers of Monopoly wish to add a new playing-piece to the board. They have offered three prototypes – a biplane, a piggybank and a money bag. They will choose, I guarantee it, the biplane. That way they will be able to continue to pretend that the most popular board game in the world for the last fifty years is just a harmless bit of fun.

To succeed in Monopoly you need greed, malice and luck. The money starts to trickle in. You corner a market. The trickle swells to a stream. Wealth breeds wealth. The stream becomes a Niagara. Once you've got the lolly, you are king and nothing holds any fears, not even jail. You just buy your way out. It's called capitalism. It's also called fascism. In the Soviet Union it was called communism. Perhaps we should just call it people.

Few joys compare with watching the dice carry a friend to your square which seethes with hotels. Friend has to mortgage his property portfolio and give you the cash. You grin. He's crippled. He ekes his life out for a few more throws and then you kill him. It's a laugh a minute.

The game ends inevitably with two tycoons lumbering round the board like dinosaurs, fixing each other with a flat dead eye. For them the world has shrunk to a board awash with property. It's Kerry Packer and Rupert Murdoch, each with enough dollar bills to light cigars for the rest of their lives.

But neither cares for money now, because they have seen through money. They know that money is just a token for something seated even deeper in the soul. That something is power. The dinosaurs circle, eyeing the jugular, probing for the chance to kill and so to reign alone, to become lords of all they survey: Mobutu, Marcos, Stalin, Ozymandias, master of the universe.

But the tycoons are blind. For when the death-blow comes and at last the victor stands alone he finds he stands atop a heap of rubble. The board has lost all meaning. Someone tips it over. The tokens of power jumble into nothingness. They are just plastic toys and bits of coloured paper. The master of the universe feels robbed. This is not what he wanted at all.

He stamps his feet. He wants another game. He rushes over to the window and shouts at the kids in the yard to come and play again. They are happy on their bicycles. They ignore him.

The bicycle game looks such fun. The master of the universe lusts to join it, but the others have glimpsed the malice in his soul. They will not let him play. He begs. He wheedles. He tries to bribe them. They laugh. The master of the universe bursts into tears.

Mum emerges to see what all the fuss is about. Mum is the Commerce Commission, the United Nations and God. She tells the children to be nice to each other. Sulkily they submit. For a while. Then someone suggests a game of Monopoly. Eyes light up.

Monopoly is us. That's why we like it. To put a piggybank or money-bag on the board would be to admit the true nature of the game. I bet you they choose the biplane.

Let the dollar fall

It is a cold wet night in June and all around the globe the bankers are butchering the kiwi dollar. Grey men with grave faces watch their millions dissolve. Even though we have seen it all before and even though we know it will pass as every crisis has passed before, gloom settles over the land.

Meanwhile in a small suburban theatre a 49-year-old insurance broker has just swaggered onto the stage dressed as a cowboy. His leggings are made of muslin decorated with black blotches so that from the back row of the stalls he appears to be wearing a pair of dead dalmatians.

> *I got spurs that jingle jangle jingle* [sings the grinning
> insurance broker]
> *As I go riding merrily along*
> *And they sing, oh ain't you glad you're single?*
> *And that song ain't so very far from wrong.*
> *O Lily-belle, O Lily-belle*
> *Though I may have done some fooling*
> *this is why I never fell;*
> *I got spurs that jingle jangle jingle*
> *And that song ain't so very far from wrong.*

The audience whoops its approval. Enter another cowboy. By day he manages an engineering company, but now on a stage in deepest suburbia he wants to

> *Ride to the ridge where the West commences;*
> *Can't look at hobbles and I can't stand fences;*
> *Don't fence me in.*

Like the insurance broker he is singing the male fantasy of freedom – except on Thursday night's performance when he and the pianist parted company. But nobody cared.

This amateur show is billed as an old-fashioned music hall. The songs come from all parts of the globe, and many of them are more a century old.

Nevertheless the 1998 audience laps them up, sings along and regularly helps the cast out with the lyrics. Why? Because they touch something fundamental. Every civilised society makes theatre because the stage holds up a mirror to our lives. It shows us our dreams and lets us laugh at them and cry at them. It brings us together. It shows us we are not alone.

While the men sing of roaming, the women (remember the age of the songs) sing of men.

'There I was, waiting at the church, waiting at the church,' trills the young lady from Avon City Ford. Her theme is echoed by the graphic designer with the wilting bouquet:

Why am I dressed in these beautiful clothes?
What is the matter with me?
I've been the bridesmaid for twenty-two brides
This time will make twenty-three.

The audience sways between sympathy and laughter.

Two ladies of mature years prance into the spotlight. One is a Justice of the Peace, the other a medical secretary, but for now both are togged up as fairies. They mourn that these days the public 'want their bit of magic from a younger bit of stuff,' and go on to explain that:

You know your days are ending
when your wand has started bending.
No one loves a fairy when she's old.

And the audience recognises the truth of the passage of time, laughs at the mirror and bellows for an encore.

But it is perhaps in the melodrama that the audience sees the world most clearly. Here life is made simple. Here good and evil fight it out. The crowd cheers the hero, hisses the villain, says aaah at the soppy bits, and laughs at everything.

Sir Ferdinand Fitzfoulenough, the wicked landlord (who in real life works for Inland Revenue), collects a bullet in the crotch, totters around the stage for well under two minutes then dies to a round of applause. The hero, Ambrose Upright (bank officer), proposes to the damsel-no-longer-in-distress (psychiatric nurse). She runs into his arms.

Last night at the very moment of her triumph, with the audience cheering and the climax looming, there rang out the unmistakable ping of snapping elastic. Instead of running, the psychiatric nurse found herself tottering towards the bank officer with a bundle of undergarments wrapped around her ankles like a squid. She tottered past the corpse of the wicked landlord. It was giggling uncontrollably.

'When we are born,' pronounced the mad King Lear, 'we cry That we are come to this great stage of fools.'

On this insignificant stage prance people who don't pretend to be anything other than fools. Nobody is paid. Nobody is serious. For the delight of an audience they play out the grand themes of life, of good and evil, of losing and finding, of loving and ageing, and they play them for sentiment and laughter. It is warm and human and funny and foolish. Something goes wrong every night and nobody cares. It is what being alive is all about.

So let the money markets do as they wish. There are things that matter far far more. Who cares that the dollar falls, so long as the curtain rises.

The Boys from Brazil

There's a town in Spain called San Sebastian where the Basque Separatists used to murder a lot of policemen. It's a beautiful place built around a bay called La Concha. At low tide the sea empties from La Concha, and on Saturdays all the men and all the boys of San Sebastian stop murdering policemen and run out on to the beach to scratch lines in the sand and put up goals and play a soccer tournament. Teams win, teams lose, legs snap, nets bulge, players hug and players weep, and then the sea returns and the players pick up their goals and go home. The sea erases the lines and irons the sand and until next Saturday La Concha belongs to the fishes.

This weekly tournament at San Sebastian is exactly like the World Cup. It differs only in scale. Like the World Cup it seems to matter hugely at the time, but it proves ephemeral. When Brazil have won the World Cup and all the hugging and weeping have died away, the tide of oblivion will sweep back in, leaving only litter on the terraces and a few Englishmen too drunk to know it's over.

Soccer is the greatest of games because it is the simplest. It is the game one instinctively plays with toddlers on the living room carpet. Add an off-side rule, a few billion spectators and an official snack bar and you've got the World Cup.

All you need to play soccer is a ball, and because the ball is round chance plays little part. What emerges is character. To play good soccer you need youth and skill. To play sublime soccer you need to be born within shooting range of the equator. Your skin must be the colour of milk chocolate or olives. You must also have only one name and it must end in 'o'. Ronaldo, for example. Or Pele.

In soccer it does not help to be white. I have just watched Holland play Brazil and none of the white Dutch players had names ending in 'o'. Their names all ended in 'donk' – apart, that is, from the chap whose entire name was Jonk. Jonk and the donks – now there's a name for a band – never had a hope. They played fine football but you could see that they were trying. What they sweated was sweat. What the Brazilians sweated was *eau de framboise au chocolat.*

The Dutch played as a team. They brought the ball upfield in beautiful neat triangles. They did what they'd been taught; but the Brazilians did what they felt. It was science against art, industry against genius, life insurance against love, beer against wine, Land-rover against Maserati, Protestant against Catholic, northern cloud against southern sun. And the sun won.

Not that the Dutch didn't have their moment. Two minutes from time their svelte black centre forward, donkless of course, rose like a cobra and headed home as sumptuous a goal as you could wish to see. But only because the Brazilians let him. They were enjoying themselves. They wanted extra time.

In the end, of course, it came down to penalties. I went to make coffee because penalties are taken by individuals. As individuals the Brazilians could not lose. I heard the cheers from the kitchen.

Brazil will win the final 2-0 but that doesn't matter. For the ninety minutes that the game lasts they will create an ephemeral beauty that will make the world gasp. After that someone will take the goalposts away and in will come the tide and the little pecking fishes.

Testosterone and tonic

Roll up, roll up. In the tent to your left, the bearded lady, to your right the rubber man, and dead ahead, sir, the fattest woman in the world. Roll up, roll up.

Those were the days. I would have rolled up to every freak show going. But nowadays the circus tents are empty. The freaks have stolen away to an even bigger circus. The freaks are playing sport.

I do not understand sumo wrestling, but I just love the wrestlers. From their dinky pony-tails to their dinky bare feet, they were made for staring at. I love those breasts like hammocks of squid, those barrel bellies, that shire-horse collar round the midriff with its worrying dangle of spikes, the audacity of those bared buttocks like the rinds of vast cheeses, those ridiculous legs, puckered monsters of cellulite atop ballet dancer ankles.

Sumos live, I gather, on sumo battery farms tended by little monks who groom them and grease them and above all feed them. I love reading lists of what the sumos eat: six bushels of rice, a hundred eggs, a cow.

Of course, the most fertile sporting field for freaks is the USA. Not so long ago a gridiron team featured a character called The Fridge. He was considerably wider than he was tall and he ran like a garage. The Fridge was cool.

Basketball's good, too, except they're all so tall you forget how tall they are. If I was in charge of basketball I would make it a law that every team had to field one short chap to remind us how tall the tall chaps are. The best basketball team ever was the Chinese Olympic team of a few years ago. Four of their five players were minuscule, but somewhere in the forests of Szechuan the authorities had found a freak. He could barely run but he dwarfed buildings. So the tactics of this wonderful team were for one player to dribble the ball around in buzzy little circles while the rest of the squad helped the arthritic colossus up the court. Once they'd stationed him beside the basket, buzzy little dribbler lobbed the ball towards the ceiling. The vast one lazily plucked the ball from the air and dropped it through the hoop.

Now, it is obvious that so long as the rules of any sport favour freaks, then that sport will be beset by drugs because drugs can aid freakishness. It is equally obvious that the war against drugs cannot be won. The drug-makers are driven by wealth and glory. The poor old drug-detectors are driven only by a sense of fair play. Wealth and glory will win every time.

So why not let them win? Let them create the freakiest freaks you ever did see by shaking up every narcotic cocktail they wish. Steroid stingers, barbiturate bombers, testosterone and tonic, let them go to it. Let the giant pharmaceuticals compete to sponsor the pharmaceutical giants.

The result will be a glorious parade of freaks for me to ogle at. It will be like the Olympics of the seventies when the East German chemists cleaned up every strength event going, apart from the women's shot-put. The latter was invariably won by the Russian chemists who had created two magnificently hairy sisters called Press. When the Presses won they wept. A thimbleful of their tears could defoliate a Siberian beech-forest.

We are constantly told that international sport these days is a global circus. Let it be a circus, then. And for those of us who do not want to pervert our bodies for a little ephemeral glory, we can continue to play beach-cricket badly for the fun of the children and not care who wins.

Moose-hunting by supermarket trolley

It's one of those Sundays. You know how it is. One of those Sundays when you can settle to nothing and the neighbours are playing the Bee Gees' Greatest Hits at full volume and the wasps of irritation in your skull say turn the telly on. So you do and there's a woman wearing a pair of athletic shorts that shouldn't be legal and she has come all the way from Latvia to New Zealand to throw the hammer. The hammer isn't a hammer, you understand, but more like one of those things used to fell mammoths from a safe distance, though it might as well be a hammer for all the good it does mankind, not that you particularly want to do mankind any good because mankind means huge women from Latvia, commentators who think hammer-throwing matters and people who like the Bee Gees.

So you zap the telly and pick up the paper only to discover that a supermarket chain has decided to make you pay a two-dollar bond on your trolley because they, poor dears, lose 200 trolleys a year and each one costs $350. At that price you immediately decide to become a trolley manufacturer and then equally immediately ditch the idea because it would lead to impossible conversations.

'Yes, that's right, yes trolleys, you know, for supermarkets … no, I don't expect you have … well, you sort of get some wire and sort of bend it … yes that's right, three good wheels and one spastic one … no, actually it *isn't* easy to make them stick together like that … ha ha, yes, mating, yes that's very funny … well, actually, about $350 each … well, it wouldn't be a very *good* second-hand car for $350, would it … yes, I know, well you can always take a basket.'

But what I really want to say is that the trolley bond will put paid to moose-hunting. Well, not exactly hunting, I suppose, more like moose-finding-by-chance. In Canada, Banff to be precise, on a skiing trip with Dave Collier way back in the days before mortgages and lady Latvians.

The après-ski at the Silver Dollar Bar and Grill has gone with a swing and about midnight we find a supermarket trolley in the street. Dave says get in, so I get in. Well, I've always been what mothers call broad in the beam, so there I am, wedged into the belly of this trolley with feet over the front and head up against the kiddy-seat and absolutely no chance of getting out without help and what with the ice on the street and Dave full of Labatt's it's a bit like the two-man bob and in ten seconds we're up to thirty miles an hour. Suddenly I see this neon motel sign with a sort of silhouette in front of it and it looks like the gigantic head of a … 'Stop!' I scream and Dave digs the heels in and says, 'why?' 'Look,' I say, 'moose.' And he says, 'Where?' and I say, 'There,' and he says, 'That's not a moose,' and I say, 'It is so,' though I don't think it is any more.

So Dave biffs a snowball at it and it turns its antlered head, bellows a sort of uniquely moosey bellow and comes charging up the street towards us.

Friendship's a great thing. Dave and I grew up together. We were inseparable. One rapidly approaching suburban moose, however, and we have discovered the joys of separability which is fine for Dave who's off up the street like a man being chased by a moose but less fine for me who has a beam wedged inextricably in the belly of a supermarket trolley. Hooves are thundering my way and I'm trying to lever myself out and wondering whether Canadian supermarket trolleys are crash-tested against two thousand pounds of moose flesh with horns and deciding they probably aren't and I am wrestling and struggling and the trolley is rocking and then ever so slowly it just topples over on its side. But my beam is still wedged so I curl like a caged foetus and pray like billyo and good old god or rather God makes the moose thunder past and head on up the street after Dave.

'Get him!' I scream, and then, quickly, 'Sorry, didn't mean it,' because I don't want him or rather Him to change his mind and make the moose do a 180.

But now, I suppose, with $2 bonds on trolleys no one will leave them around any more, so yet another source of fun will dissolve in what is becoming a puritan world, but at least moose will be able to browse in peace.

Meanwhile gangs of horror-children will hang around in super-market carparks with their skateboards and their hideous haircuts and when some poor pensioner wheels the groceries out to the Honda Civic, whack! it'll be a skateboard on the bonce and a horizontal pensioner and the kids will be off with the trolley, and all for two lousy bucks.

So I suppose the supermarket will have to hire carpark guards, and what better than a vast lady Latvian with a penchant for ham-mer-throwing? The urchins will evaporate, and if some itinerant moose happens to wander into the carpark she could let rip with the hammer and a great Latvian grunt and take its legs out from under it.

Dave got away, by the way. He always did.

Erratum
Due to typesetting difficulties the word 'France' was repeatedly mis-spelt as 'Brazil' in the column on the World Cup. My apologies.

Fun and games

In the town where I was brought up all games took place at the recreation ground. Indeed it held something for almost everyone; the recreation ground was virtually a metaphor for life itself.

At one end stood the kiddies' playground, hilariously close to the main road, where junior citizens amused themselves by falling off the swings onto the concrete that the council had thoughtfully laid beneath. Next to the playground stood the War Memorial Gardens, to which the kiddies graduated when things began to happen to their bodies. Teenage couples would disappear into this dense and litter-strewn shrubbery for lengthy games of doctors and nurses. When they emerged they got married and joined the cricket club.

The cricket ground, of course, lay beside the War Memorial Gardens, and it was into those gardens that every local batsman strove to hit the ball. It was revenge for lost youth.

Into the rhododendrons went the ball and out came a yelp. Moments later there would scurry from the undergrowth a girl in a state of partial undress pursued by a boy in a state of complete frustration. On a fine day in high summer one could sometimes flush out as many as three couples with a single lofted on-drive. It was like dropping a ferret into a rabbit warren.

The target for batsmen at the other end was the bowling green. Land a cricket ball like a mortar in the middle of the bowls players and shortly afterwards you heard the ambulance. Clutching their tickers the ancient ones fell in concentric circles as if the ball was the epicentre of a nuclear blast.

The bowls players, however, never minded being used as targets since before their bodies betrayed them, they too had played cricket. They accepted the transition from hunter to hunted as part of the great scheme of things.

They knew, as well, that bowls wasn't a sport, but rather a pastime. It got them out and about and gave a little gentle exercise to withered limbs. Furthermore it staved off the day when they would toddle across the road from the recreation ground for the last time and pass through the grim portals of the Adastra Rest Home.

From there, it was just a short totter to the premises of Guttam, Washam & Plant.

Once upon a time, then, a thoughtful young man could stand with chin in hand beside the recreation ground and see his life mapped out for him from playground to graveyard. It was a strangely comforting vision, like the rhythm of the seasons. It sang of continuity.

But how all that has changed. The old certainties have crumbled, and one of the first to go was the game of bowls. Despite being designed as the simplest and gentlest of games to allow for the frailties of age it has been hijacked.

These days the oldies can only stand aside and gawp as fit young things in tracksuits strut around the green and run after their bowls and squeal with excitement and care who wins. Such people are grave robbers. They will come to very sticky ends, of course, but that does little to console the elderly whose gentle recreation has been taken from them.

Of course, once bowls had become a professional sport, the dam of common sense had burst and the waters of absurdity flooded through the breach. These days it is possible to earn one's living from playing darts, or snooker, or water-skiing, or ten-pin bowling, or any one of a thousand brands of motor-racing, each as hideous and senseless as the other.

Who pays these people to play their games? I cannot tell you. Who watches them play? I cannot tell you. Where will it end? I cannot tell you that either. All I can tell you for sure is that with the bowlers of today and the fish-throwers of tomorrow walks the strange and spectral figure of the twenty-first century.

The anagrams of God

I, too, am a victim. The dog was asleep when my tennis ball stopped beside it. The dog woke to find me apparently making a grab for its testicles. It bit my wrist. I was seven years old, and so, as it happens, was the dog.

The dog's owners drove me to hospital in their admirable open-topped MG and bought me a Heart ice-cream which I'd never had before because they cost a shilling. I presume I had a tetanus jab but don't remember it. But I do remember spending the rest of my childhood rolling tennis balls hopefully towards sleeping dogs.

Last week a dog killed a man. The anti-dog lobby has gone rabid. With just the sort of cool, detached reasoning that did so much for Yugoslavia, they are slavering at the bar of public opinion and calling for fierce new laws to quell the canine menace.

In search of the true scale of the problem I studied a recent issue of the local newspaper. It contained thirty-seven accounts of human misery. These I divided into four sections: misery caused by people; misery caused by God; misery caused by dogs; and misery caused by goats. People beat God 34 – 2. The dogs failed to score. The goats notched a single spectacular goal.

My dog Jessie loves everyone. Jessie even loves golfers. In the urge to serve the merry golfers of Hagley Park, Jessie will leap into the rough to retrieve their muffed drives. The merry golfers roar like stags and wave their graphite shafts. And well they might, because the golfers of Hagley Park know that golf matters; some of them indeed have handicaps comfortably under thirty. Not for them the cheerful self-deprecating laugh. One of them once took to Jessie with a four-iron.

You see, the dog-haters and the Tiger Woodses of Hagley have something in common: they've got the world sussed. They know what's what. They are civilised and they have got it right. The rest of creation has got it wrong. Dogs merely sleep and eat and love their owners. Dogs play games but they don't fill out their score-cards properly and they forget who won. They show enthusiasm and they shit without embarrassment. They own nothing and like sex and never hold grudges and love to serve and are grateful for all affection and don't judge. No wonder the four-irons scythe the air. No wonder people hate dogs.

The irrefutable statistical truth is that if something kills your child, that something will be a person or God. Not a dog. The one case brought against a dingo was thrown out of court.

Admittedly goats do get the odd child but not enough to be statistically significant.

Mankind invented virtue. We have built pulpits from which to preach forgiveness, loyalty, honesty and love. Yet if we anatomise man our scalpel discovers vanity, acquisitiveness, deceit and golf.

I have not met a vain dog, nor an acquisitive one, nor yet a deceitful one, and only a few who play golf. Dogs forgive. They are loyal. They are honest. They love. And for the very few who are bad there are already perfectly adequate laws to control them.

I would point out to the dog-haters and the hackers of Hagley that there are five anagrams of God and surely it is no coincidence that one of them is ogd. There's also dgo, gdo and odg. I have never owned any of these.

But I have owned dogs. My dogs know nothing. Unlike me they don't imagine they know anything. My dogs are happier, better and wiser than I shall ever be.

Communing with shags

I've never had any time for the sceptics of this world who don't believe in telepathy. Life, you see, is contact with people, any sort of contact. 'Only connect,' said E.M. Forster. And if you think that's hooey, try playing the hermit for a fortnight and then get back to me. Or rather don't.

But if life is all about contact, what do you do when your telepathy is picking up only static, the e-mail has crashed, the letter-box is empty, everyone you ring is out or dead or both and there's a knock at the door from Sister Solitude and her pale and silent daughter Loneliness? I don't know about you, but I go and look at shags. There is solace in shags.

'Come on, dogs,' I say and we bound to the door, our tails walloping the crockery.

Round Lyttelton the shags roost in a couple of clifftop conifers, and very decorative they look, too, with their plump white breasts, one to a bird, and their necks like those bits of plumbing under the sink.

But it is not for their looks that I visit the shags, nor for the way they gurgle like outboard motors, nor indeed for the comfort of their brute insensibility. I go to laugh at them for being called shags.

They bring to mind a boy I went to school with called Tinker, which may not be the best of surnames, but there are worse, several of which end in bottom. Tinker, however, was christened Simon. There are worse names than Simon too, but few worse than S. Tinker.

Then there was the little Egyptian boy whom I taught and who was called Fallik. He was only seven, the poor dear. And so very cheerful. It made one weep.

Anyway, off to the shags we go for a giggle, and it's a wild night. Clouds scud, trees thrash, and King Lear would have felt at home. The dogs disappear into the bush in yelping pursuit of imaginary prey, the night swallows them, and I am alone among the thrashing trees and the scudding clouds and the eerie dark.

I've always been a gutsy bloke, especially when alone in the bush on stormy nights, so even though I can hear the footsteps of an axe-murderer on the path behind me I just chuckle a nonchalant chuckle and carry on shagwards with my pulse comfortably under 200. And there I am, humming a catchy little Leonard Cohen number about suicide and the sea is crashing at the foot of the cliff and I'm thinking thoughts when whoompha, SOMETHING comes flying out of the darkness, headbutts my thigh and disappears over the cliff to certain death.

I react calmly. It is the work of only a few moments to locate my heart under a pittosporum, dust it off and slip it back in. Then I gather my wits. A couple of the more timid wits are gibbering behind boulders, but when all are safely gathered I set about seeking a rational explanation of the assault on my thigh, and of course there is a rational explanation; viz, I have just been attacked by an alien.

Well, good to have sorted that one out. The walk ends without further drama. Naturally, however, my mind chews over this encounter with a thigh-butting kamikaze Venusian.

And I recall a story I heard the other night from a learned gentleman in a hotel on the Lyttelton waterfront. It is a story of Russian science. (Be patient now; this will all come together.)

What the clever Russians did was to take half a dozen baby rabbits on a cruise to the bottom of the Baltic Sea in a submarine. Then they killed them.

Meanwhile, and here's the cunning part, up on dry land, other Russians sank electrodes into the mother rabbit's brain to measure the synaptic polarity of her ganglions. And sure enough, as each of her little brood was garrotted fifty fathoms below decks, there was a measurable discharge of protons. And if that doesn't prove the truth of telepathy and I don't know what else, but probably homeopathy, I'll eat a sceptic's hat.

Now, as you know, Lyttelton is currently home to a sad gang of Russian sailors stranded here through no fault of their own. And I have no doubt that in their sadness they often take a stroll along the cliffs to cheer themselves up with a treeful of shags.

One thing I have noticed about Russians is that they look remarkably like human beings. So, from about 10am most days, do I. The point of all this is that down by the cliffs on a stormy night, what with the clouds scudding, trees thrashing, etc., it would be easy to mistake me for a Russian. And that, of course, is exactly what happened.

The thing that assaulted my thigh was no Venusian. It was a rabbit. A rabbit, furthermore, which was telepathically aware of the cruelties its fellow rabbits had suffered on the other side of the world and which was bent on revenge against the race that had done it to them.

Although the rabbit failed in its mission, and may well have perished, I think it all rather moving. Here was a rabbit that connected. Here was a rabbit that felt itself to be a part of the greater scheme of things. Here was a rabbit that laid down its life for its friends. Which of us can lay his hand on his heart and say he does not envy that rabbit its fate?

Life is contact.

P.C. Sturrock

On the morning when both my dogs were simultaneously, spectacularly and indeed voluminously sick in the car, police buttocks shone from the front page of my newspaper. And all this at a time when the police were marching in search of a pay rise. It would have been easy to conclude that the world was coming to an end.

Now, there are several points that need to be made here, but first, for reasons that should become clear, I need to introduce you to a boy with whom I went to school.

This boy had all the charm of dog-sick. He wore shorts in the fifth form. Nobody else did. It was agreed among the schoolboys of England that to wear shorts beyond the age of twelve was a sign of effeminacy, lunacy or both, which was exactly why this boy did it. He longed for people to say, 'You are wearing shorts, which means you are an effeminate lunatic,' because then he could kill them.

He terrified me, and even now I hesitate to name him. But perhaps at forty it is time for me to take my spindly courage in both hands. His name (come closer now; I am typing softly) was Sturrock.

Sturrock's greatest pleasure was Bawden. Bawden was a skinny child who never once called Sturrock an effeminate lunatic. Nevertheless, Sturrock regularly used to cram him into sports lockers the size of nesting boxes. On more creative days he would casually tie Bawden's limbs into a knot and place him on top of a cupboard like an ornament. When the ornament squealed Sturrock grinned.

At the end of the fifth form Sturrock decided there was little fun left in stirring the rubble of Bawden's psyche and he left school in search of fresh woods and pastures new. Driven no doubt by the wish to continue beating people up without being punished for it, Sturrock applied to join the police force.

Now, I do not know whether Sturrock became a copper, but for the sake of Great Britain I hope he didn't. Sturrock was not the sort of human being who took kindly to being asked the time.

Which brings us to the question of what sort of human beings police officers should be. The answer to that is extraordinary people. Armed only with the right to use the minimum force required to uphold the law, they are required to walk towards situations that instinct tells them to run away from.

They are required to accept insults but not bribes, to do as they are bid whether or not they agree with the instruction, to treat people whom they do not like in exactly the same way as they treat people whom they do like, and as a matter of routine to deal with the sordid and the sad, the brutal and the bloody. At rugby matches they must stand with their backs to the game.

In other words, they are required to behave unnaturally. They are paid to embody our better selves, to represent our civic conscience, the side of us that knows the way things ought to happen, to enforce the laws which we have elected people to Parliament to make. Having a police force is like paying someone to make us keep our New Year resolutions. They are not paid much to do it, and it cannot be much fun.

And then, behold, on the front page of the paper, a photograph of policemen having a lot of fun. In order to raise funds for their Dragon Boat team they are stripping off mock uniforms to the delight of a sizeable crowd.

The obvious point is that the police officers concerned were off duty. At work a police officer is required to be as rational as Mr Spock. Off duty he is allowed to have red blood in his veins; he is allowed to love and to laugh and to drink and to be wrong. And if he wants to remove his clothes in a night-club for a laugh, I am not at all surprised. It might help him tomorrow when he has to deal with someone who prefers removing the clothes from other people and then raping them.

Without the police the world would be an unfair place. If tonight the police all folded their tents and crept out of town, looting would begin within the hour, John Citizen would buy a gun tomorrow morning, the suburban vigilantes would be formed by afternoon tea and by lunchtime on Friday there would be anarchy. You and I, dear reader, could be dead.

In most countries of the world, the police are corrupt. Here, on the whole, they are not. No doubt the New Zealand police force contains the odd Sturrock but by and large the police act as they should; they guard the system by which we have chosen to govern ourselves.

In sum, then, the fuss over the strip show is wrong-headed and the fuss over pay is important. The police should be paid what they want and then some. The profession of policing should be so attractive that good and talented people queue to enter it.

Then when Sturrock emigrates to come looking for me and decides to do a little policing while he is here to keep his hand in, the recruiting officer can show him the door. With any luck Sturrock will kick it, whereupon he will be arrested.

Meanwhile, if you are seeking a Subaru Omega in good running order and fragrance is not a consideration, I might be able to help.

The ods roll over

As a child my main joy was watching the car's odometer. Of course, in those innocent pre-metric days we called it the milometer; back then we barely knew what an od was. Nevertheless, what I craved was that moment when the odometer numbers all rolled round together to produce a row of zeros.

Not daring to blink, I would follow the odometer's slow progress through the 990s. I would urge my father to drive faster, but he would decline on the grounds that top gear was for hooligans.

In the end, of course, it turned out like the weather forecast. Just as, however closely you listen to the weather forecast you always seem to miss the bit you want, so somehow I always seemed to miss the great odometer roll. One moment of distraction and 999.7 was suddenly 1000.1.

Immediately I would order my father to reverse. He would refuse, partly because he didn't believe in pandering to children, but mainly because he despised reverse. He called it the foreigners' gear.

Why do I mention all this? Partly to show modern youth that in my day we knew how to make our own fun, but more because it has something to do with the end of a year. Tonight at midnight the globe's odometer ticks over a notch and it matters.

Here in the port tonight those people who can wrench themselves away from The Moira Anderson Hogmanay Special will tour the pubs. There are several pubs here. In them will gather a cosmopolitan mix. There will be gold-toothed Russian trawlermen smelling of the fierce disinfectant used to kill cockroaches on board their awful ships. There will be Koreans and Vietnamese, wharfies and rugmakers, emigre artists and Arthur the bee-keeper side by side in a seething mass.

A billion words will be shouted or slurred across tables awash with slops. Few of the words will be heard but that doesn't matter. It's the doing of it that will count, the being there.

I am told that when women share a house, their biorhythms gradually merge until eventually they find they are all pedalling their menstrual cycles in time with each other. So it is with the revellers at New Year's Eve in the port. As the evening wears on this ruck of humanity becomes like a school of fish. It develops an unconscious group will. Without anyone saying anything, all the revellers decide at more or less the same time to move to the next pub. One minute a bar will be bulging till its walls groan; the next it will be a wasteland of glasses, ashtrays and nobody. If you get out of phase with the mob you wonder if you've got the date wrong.

As midnight looms a crowd gathers at the corner of Oxford and London Streets. There is a sense in the air of something important, something ritualistic and significant. A ship's siren blasts the night. A cheer erupts, and the people join hands to sing Auld Lang Syne with such tunefulness that every dog in town joins in.

Then it's hugs. Some hug only their lovers; others, like random octopuses, hug anyone within range; while a few sly youths hug the girls they've have spent the past year wanting to hug. And that is apt because New Year's Eve is a vent for feelings that spend the rest of the year deep in the burrows of reserve.

The mob drifts apart. Those who threw away their cigarettes at midnight nip back to the pub to replace them. Those who emerged from the rusting trawlers return to them singing. Those who came down from the hills stumble gently back up towards home. Halfway up the slope they may pause to catch breath, and perhaps, encouraged by the twinkle of the lights and the dark of the sea and the black presence of the hills, they will reflect on the passage of time, the year that has gone, the year that is to come.

For that, I think, is what this ritual of New Year's Eve is all about. It is a marker-post stuck down at random along the great amorphous road of time. It serves the same function as a birth or a marriage or a death. And like those occasions it arouses sentimentality.

For some that sentiment is the mawkishness of televisual Hogmanay; for others it's the euphoria of the hug; for me I'm afraid
it's a grim little poem.

> *Life is mainly froth and bubble.*
> *Two things stand as stone:*
> *Kindness in another's trouble,*
> *Courage in one's own.*

Every New Year's Eve this hideous doggerel rises unbidden to my
mind. And every year, softened by beer, I resolve that henceforth
I shall be kinder and more courageous. And having so resolved I
meander the last few ods to home and grateful bed.

The resolution, of course, comes to nothing, but it's the thought
that counts. Happy New Year.

Drinking rituals

Life is a sentence punctuated by rituals. The only thing the rituals have in common is drink.

The weddings start at somewhere around twenty and go on for about a decade. Of one's friends it tends to be the sexually avid who marry first. Two days after he left university, my mate Freddy, as groin-driven as any man you could hope, or possibly not hope, to meet, married a monoglot Pole. He didn't want conversation to interfere with the true purpose of marriage.

The wedding was a magnificent affair. Boatloads of bulky Poles came over for the binge, bringing with them a serious devotion to having a good time and a solution to the language barrier. This solution came in several crates of clear bottles with handwritten labels. Over the course of a weekend so memorable that none of us can remember any of it, I learned more than enough Polish to get by in Poland. The Polish for vodka is vodka.

Joy was so utterly let off the leash at Freddy's wedding that it not only carved holes in the liver but also rather spoiled me for subsequent weddings. Nevertheless it established a pattern that proved true of them all.

Every wedding bears an undertow of grief to which women are more sensitive than men, perhaps because they know more about affairs of the heart, or perhaps because they are more likely to be sober. It's something to do with the unmarried ones wanting to be married, and with the knowledge that the newly-made wife has got a lot of work in front of her taming the beast to whom she has now hitched her wagon.

Parents are always sad. If the tosh about not losing a daughter but gaining a son-in-law weren't tosh they wouldn't cry so much. Daughter is firmly lost and the son-in-law has the table manners of a skunk. Had daughter not developed an inexplicable and un-dissuadable crush on the thug they wouldn't have given him house-room.

The critical moment at a wedding is the departure of bride and groom swamped with hugs, flowers and smut. Someone has tied cans to the car. Beer cans. Symbols of bachelorhood. As the car pulls off they rattle at the back of the groom's skull like the tug of the past, like the tinkle of the jailer's key. Just round the corner the car stops and he leaps out to detach them, having first checked that there is no beer left in any of them. There isn't. Life has changed.

Meanwhile back at the ritual the women wave at the invisible car for about two hours and then turn to look at each other, a sisterhood of wonder. The men do the same, except the wave lasts two seconds and the look one. Then they sprint to the bar. Now's the time for some serious wedding.

As the years pass the invitations dwindle. The last pair of your acquaintance to marry are the bookish sort. She wears hairgrips, he a cardigan. It is a quiet affair. There is parsnip wine, but not enough to dull the pain.

After the weddings come the christenings. These are splendid bashes, which the children are mercifully still too bloblike to ruin. Women compare husbands and babies; husbands compare baldness. Hooch flows almost as strongly as the lies about the past.

The only downside to christenings is godfathership. God and fatherhood are among my weaker suits and yet several friends have asked me to do the job. I presume they imagined I would be good for presents. By now they know better.

As one descends into middle age the rituals drop off. For a while. But I got an invite this morning in a richly thick envelope. The card inside had a black deckle edging. I hope there will be drink.

Fine words, coffee and parsnips

Since Roman times they've been saying silly things about wine – *'in termino vanillae et tarmaci hintus'** – that sort of stuff, and no one has paid any attention. Wine has continued to do its principal job of making you say regrettable things at dinner parties. Now, however, and this is serious, the high priests of pretension have got their claws into coffee.

Coffee is a simple thing and good. Of a morning it prises apart the eyelids and unbends the fingers. At work it soothes the troubled breast. It makes the ideal accompaniment to 15 cigarettes. It's bad for you. These are great virtues.

But now there is bafflement abroad. I quote verbatim a conversation recently overheard:

Waitperson: 'Welcome, sir, to our unpretentious brasserie somewhere in the trendy bit of the city. My name is Gustave. I am your waitperson for today. You may admire my pony-tail. What can I do for you, sir?'

Jurassic Man: 'A cup of coffee.'

Waitperson (barely suppressing a giggle): 'I beg your pardon, sir.'

Jurassic Man: 'A cup of coffee.'

Waitperson (patronisingly, for it has now dawned on him that he is dealing with Jurassic Man): 'Do you perchance mean a Latte with an acute accent, sir? Or perhaps a Cappuccino with a random number of p's and c's and a sprinkle of cinnamon to disguise the flavour of coffee, which barely exists anyway because of the three inches of industrial froth. Or perhaps a Short Black is what you seek, sir, with or without racial jokes. Or maybe a Long Flat White, sir, a name we used to ascribe to a tall drunken friend at university. Or yet again you could be after one of those little french thimbles of espresso palate-stripper.'

At this point Jurassic Man realises he has several options. Option one is to insist on just an ordinary cup of coffee, in which case he will receive the bitter dregs from a Cona machine last operated on Monday. Option two is to strike the waitperson. Option three is to stand on his dignity. Standing on the dignity is hard work when in need of a cup of coffee, but it does grant a good vantage point from which to strike the waitperson.

They've sunk their claws into food, too. Have you read the menu? There's poetry there. You used to get pork. Now it's medallions of pork. This translates as much less pork than you'd like. You are consoled, however, by the hint that the pig served valiantly in the war or won the pole-vault at school.

Further consolation comes from knowing that the dead pig is comfortable. No longer does it come with rice. It now nestles on a bed of the stuff, snoring gently no doubt and dreaming of storming machine-gun posts or soaring over the bar against a cloudless sky to the ecstatic grunts of a worldwide television audience of a billion sows.

To pamper it yet further while nestling on its *ris*, the pig has been drizzled with a warm *jus*. I like the sound of that. I'm going to hire someone to come to my bedroom nightly and drizzle me with warm *jus*. I shall charge people to watch. Perhaps the watchers might like to contribute by brushing me with a coriander and honey glaze. I shall reassure them that neither the glaze nor the drizzle of warm *jus* will affect my flavour in the least. Only my price.

Vegetables have gone, of course. The three vegies of yesteryear now arrive as a polenta. That translates as a mess. Or a roulade, meaning a mess. Or a terrine. That means a mess. Or a compote. That means a compost. My primary school lunch-lady had mastered the compote in the early 1960s. She called it mashed swede. Dave Collier used to sneak it out of the dining hall in his pockets to throw at buses. A well-aimed handful could cover a whole windscreen.

As I say, wine's fine. They can say what they like about wine. But it seems that now, like the Anglican church, the pretentious are no longer content in their traditional temples. They are aiming for outreach into the community. They are not welcome.

In the end, it all boils down to words. He was a wise and good man who said a long time ago that fine words butter no parsnips. He might have added that they make a lousy cup of coffee.

---

*'in the finish a hint of vanilla and asphalt'

A place of worship

The Rebel Sports building beats it, of course, and so, perhaps, does the Tower Building in the Square, but the Christchurch Casino is nevertheless an impressively ugly building. Its exterior resembles a medieval fortress by NASA out of Picasso, and is indeed so ugly that it is sure to have won international design awards.

The interior of the casino is not so much ugly as absurd, a hotchpotch of oriental, Egyptian, Roman, Edwardian and fairground tack. Fake gold abounds. Fairy lights flicker. It's like Disneyland without the cultural depth.

But we who push through its revolving glass doors don't give a pound of parsnips about what it looks like; our minds are on higher things. We wish only to sidestep security, to mount the marble stairs and to start tossing money away.

In an astute psychological ploy the casino has banned jeans. Parties you can't go to are of course the parties to go to, thus the casino becomes hugely attractive to those of us who wear jeans. So we ditch the denim, pull on the Dress-For-Less slacks and, hey presto!, we've gatecrashed the party, become members of a club that doesn't want us as members and we feel good.

The casino sucks a mass of men and women through its doors, but, once inside, the sexes split. Men tend to head for the card tables where the opposition has a face. This face belongs to a croupier who wears a cummerbund from Curtain City but is nevertheless young, polite, sober, good at maths and has the odds of every game stacked in his favour. He's an obvious pushover.

For now we are at the table we have transcended our everyday selves. Just as children dress up to become superheroes like Batman and Richard Long, so, dressed for less at the five-dollar blackjack table, we men become Minnesota Fats, Sydenham Sid and Good-time Lou of Lyttelton.

We love the ritual. We also love to be seen to know the ritual, proud to be familiar with a safely sleazy underworld. In our minds we have donned green sun-visors and the smoke from our plump cigars is wreathing beneath a lowered lamp shade. We flick imperious fingers and call for a beer. Shaken, not stirred.

Women, on the other hand, generally avoid the card tables. Instead they poke the pokies. Many theories exist on why they do this. According to Professor Collier (*Westport Journal of Psychology*, vol. 1, p.3) 'women, being of a less combative and more co-operative disposition, are averse to the sensation of potentially depriving the croupier/child figure of his or her visible means of support.' Or it may just be that most women don't know the rules of blackjack.

You can eat at the casino, too, of course, and inevitably the meal that Seb the Chef produces is a smorgasbord. For the casino is Enid Blyton country, the land at the top of the Faraway Tree, the land of Take What You Want. To push through those posh doors is to leave the workaday world behind. The temperature is constant. The light is constant. There are no windows to grant us a glimpse of the grim beyond, and no clocks to taunt us with the tyranny of time.

When the casino first rose to sully the Christchurch skyline some people said it would fail. What they meant was that they hoped it would fail. It was never going to fail. Casinos don't fail. They are built on the sturdiest of foundations.

The first foundation stone is greed, of course, and the second is vanity. Consumed by self-importance we imagine that this is our lucky day. We ignore the other punters thronging the tables, all of whom imagine it is their lucky day as well. Something in the back of our psyches whispers to us that the universe is built around us alone and Lady Luck just loves us.

One of the most noticeable things about the casino is how quiet it is, how little conversation takes place. Transfixed by pokey screens or the flicking fingers of the croupier, the gambling congregation silently lays open its wallet at the feet of fortune and emits a barely audible hum. It is the hum of prayer.

So perhaps my opening image was wrong. The casino is not so much a fortress as a church, a church dedicated to that most ancient of goddesses, probability theory. Like all churches it exists because hope is stronger than reason, because the world is an unsatisfactory place and because we are human. See you there Sunday?

Bounce me

The trouble with Auckland bouncers is that they don't bounce. Last week, on the eve of my forty-first birthday, I snuck out from behind the Tweed Curtain of Christchurch, and took my first jaunt to the Queen City, City of Sails. I saw few queens and no sails, but I did glimpse the inside of a bar or two.

Within an hour of arrival we were seated in a top-notch bar, much patronised, I was told, by the beautiful. You could tell the place was top-notch because its title consisted entirely of consonants like the top line of one of those optician's eye-charts. Furthermore, the walls were unpainted, the floor bare, the furniture built of reinforcing steel and two beers cost the same as a drab but serviceable ownership flat in Invercargill.

It was less easy to tell that the patrons were beautiful. Maybe it was the lighting, kept low to conceal the menu prices. I did make out, however, that whenever the door opened, every face turned to assess the entrant for fame and beauty. When Pete pointed out a chap who had done several episodes of *Shortland Street* I realised the expense was worth it. I also resolved to start gelling my hair.

Dismounting the reinforcing steel we headed into Ponsonby to continue life's quest for cheaper beer. We found it – we could hardly fail to – in an altogether more pub-like pub called something reassuring like The Pig and Chisel. The Pig and Chisel served Guinness. It took a while to leave.

The bouncer at the doors of the Casino told me flatly that I was swaying. I wasn't. I was rocking rhythmically though an arc of about 30 degrees. I told him the harrowing tale of my middle-ear defect which has affected my balance on and off for over twenty years, mainly at weekends. And this Casino darling, he of the brutal face, became the first bouncer in all that time to swallow my middle ear, as it were.

I am extremely good at blackjack. I told Pete. Pete suggested I should go easy. I told Vladimir, the croupier on the blackjack table. Vladimir smiled that queasy smile that croupiers smile when they know they've met a punter who's got them licked. 'See,' I said to Pete, 'Vladimir knows.'

I did not know that there are daily cash limits on ANZ Night and Day cash withdrawal cards. Mine is $500. I reached it in twenty minutes. I gave the final $20 to Pete to fritter away. He took it to that graveyard of fools, the roulette table, and turned it rapidly into $170. This, with great good grace and generosity of spirit, I took back from Pete so I could have another go at Vlad the Impaler.

I decided in the end it was all the bouncer's fault. Nevertheless it's a surprisingly refreshing feeling to find oneself on the eerie streets of a strange city at four in the morning on one's forty-first birthday with absolutely no money and no way of getting any. So long, that is, as Pete has enough for a nightcap and a taxi.

The bouncer in the only hotel bar we could find open was reading the New Testament. Auckland was rapidly becoming a city of firsts. The bouncer, as gently as one would expect from a man of God, let us know that we couldn't come in unless we were hotel guests. It was Pete's idea to tell him we were the hired entertainment. It was the bouncer's astonishing idea to let us in. It was mine to sing 'Nessun Dorma'.

As you know, the second line of the melody has some rather tricky arpeggios. We needed bouncing. It's to do with self-respect. Don't Auckland bouncers understand that?

In the end we had to bounce ourselves.

Nothing doing

At this time of the year letter-boxes and television screens are awash with advertisements for holidays. All of them are advertising the same destination, that eternally attractive location called Somewhere Else.

The attraction of Somewhere Else is that it isn't where you are. In Somewhere Else there is always heat, sand and a girl in a white bikini. Where you are there is cold, concrete and the extraordinary woman next door.

The girl in Somewhere Else spends most of her time swimming in limpid lagoons. She always does the breaststroke. Advertisers seem to like the way that makes her legs move. The woman next door has never been known to do the breaststroke. She does not look as if she would be very good at it.

The point about Somewhere Else is that when you are there you don't have to do anything. In Somewhere Else work is something that other people do. The idea of such indolence appeals to us.

Unfortunately, doing nothing is only interesting when there's something you should be doing. If I have an article to write or a pile of exercise books to mark there is nothing so delicious as slumping in the armchair with my feet on the windowsill and gawping out of the window. Clouds become fascinating. Once the words are written or the books marked, clouds are clouds.

In Somewhere Else your job is to lie on the beach, drink things with umbrellas in them and look for the girl in the white bikini. Ten minutes of this and you've found out that the things with umbrellas in cost a lot of money, your skin is reddening nicely, the sisters of the extraordinary woman next door have chosen the same place as you to go on holiday and are indeed proving that the family cannot do breaststroke, and the girl in the white bikini isn't there. Perhaps she has gone on holiday. In fact, she is probably looking for someone like you in the place you have just come from.

You turn over to cook the other side of your flesh. There's a faint tearing sound as your skin separates from the nylon lounger and you realise with stunning clarity that you're bored. There are ten days of holiday to go.

I met a mother of six the other day. She's one of those wonder-women. While nursing a sick child under one arm and arbitrating a squabble between two others, she's cooking fishfingers for the horde and preparing chicken chasseur for an adult dinner party after the kids have gone to bed. In her spare moments she runs an employment agency.

On Mother's Day this year her family presented her with a week's holiday in Fiji. On her own. She burst into tears of gratitude, hugged each of them for five minutes and said she didn't want to go. They wouldn't hear of it.

Before she went she crammed two weeks' work into one week to make sure everyone could survive her absence. When her family put her onto the plane she was exhausted. Nevertheless she spent the flight worrying. Somewhere over the Pacific she seriously considered going to the cockpit to tell the pilot to turn around. Taking a grip, she convinced herself that things would be better when she arrived.

On her first day she swam, played tennis, went pony-trekking and thoroughly cleaned her hotel room. On the second day she hung around the creche until someone asked her if she would like to lend a hand. On the third day she came home.

The lure of holidays is the lure of fantasy. What spoils them is the one item of luggage that no one tells us to pack but which we carry with us everywhere we go.

The tourists are coming

Shhh, now. Listen.

What you can hear on the wind is the distant clamour of tourists. In Tashkent and in Tokyo, in Seoul and in Sydney the tourists of the world are clamouring for one thing only. They are clamouring for Brighton Pier.

That wail you can hear is the grief of a Korean tycoon; he has found that all flights to Brighton are booked a year ahead. That whoop is the whoop of a Japanese millionaire; he has booked a suite at the Hotel Ocean Vista, New Brighton. That thwack is the thwack of the mugger's truncheon. The millionaire falls to the Tokyo pavement. The mugger melts into the night, a hotel-booking fluttering in his fingers.

Of course, in the race for the tourist dollar Brighton has always kept its nose in front of humdrum places like Bali. The beautiful people have always come to Brighton. On arrival the beautiful people have traditionally disguised themselves as solitary middle-aged women, rented a dog, and gone to the beach to throw sticks.

Brighton has everything – golden beaches, a Mitre 10, and just up the road a Night of Maori Magic. But what sets Brighton apart, its ineffable *je ne sais quoi*, is that in Brighton the clocks stopped in 1974.

As Stratford harks back to Shakespeare, and Rome to Julius Caesar, so Brighton harks back to Saturday shopping. Brighton is frozen in the era of those free-standing ashtrays which whizz when you press them. It's nylon carpet country. If you tilt your nostrils just so in Brighton you can catch the whiff of lava-lamps.

But not content with Brighton's nostalgic charms the city fathers have sought to make Brighton even more desirable. They have gathered round the whizzing ashtray, sucked hard on their

Pocket Edition and from amid the fug have come up with an idea so novel that nobody else has come up with it since 1893. They have built a pier.

And what a pier. Not for Brighton the traditional seaside fripperies of shelter or entertainment, paint or purpose. This pier is a pier. It is built of concrete disguised as concrete. On this pier you can walk to the end. Nothing gets in your way. Then you can walk back. No wonder the tourists clamour to plant their Guccis on it.

But even that is not all. Having built the greatest tourist attraction since the giant plastic kiwifruit, the city fathers have gone one better. To pamper the jet-set they have decided to add that ultimate indulgence, a lending library. One can only applaud the daring and the vision. Brighton's future bulges with promise.

And yet I believe the city fathers have erred. If only they had put the sea between the residents of Brighton and their books. If only they had put the library at the far end of the pier.

Picture the joys. It is an August morning. The easterly howls. As the gates of the pier open, the zimmer-framed ones surge forwards, lusting for literature. They are bent against the wind. Under their arms they clutch large-print Georgette Heyers. Under their shoes the great grey widow-maker rears and crashes against the concrete piles. The daily race to reach the library has begun.

Meanwhile, in the air-conditioned penthouse suites of a hundred sea-front hotels the tourist hordes train high-powered binoculars and place their bets. Millions of yen have gone on the little old lady in the purple raincoat.

A sudden squall of wind. Two umbrellas become parachutes and off into the Pacific flies another pair of pensioners. The tourists gasp as one, then sigh with relief as they see that the purple raincoat has not faltered. Although the breakers become thick with a bobbing mass of the literate elderly, the purple raincoat trudges on against the wind, urged forward by prayers to a thousand Asian Gods.

Now that really would bring the crowds to Brighton.

The discontent of our winter

I'm a rudely healthy chap but once a winter I wake to a wet pillow. It happened last week.

During the night, fluids I couldn't name and didn't want to had seeped from my head. In addition, a tadpole had lodged in my throat, a tadpole that grew within hours into the mother of all frogs with a croak like a V8. By lunchtime the cold had blossomed into a phlegm-fest.

The cold may be common but it brings with it a vocabulary of rare beauty. Consider the congestion of catarrh. Or the music of mucus. Or the slither of sputum. And is there a more wondrously onomatopoeic word in the language than phlegm? With its cluster of slimy consonants and its brilliant silent g, phlegm sings of ill-health.

At this point I would like to stress that neither I nor any member of my immediate family has ever expressed the opinion that Mucus, Sputum and Phlegm would be a good title for a firm of solicitors.

I live most of the year without sinuses. Then suddenly I have them to burn, and every one a phlegm-factory on overtime. The more I clear their product the more I encourage them to act as the source of the great grey-green greasy Limpopo River.

Nevertheless there are joys to having a cold. The first of these is that I cannot taste my own cooking. You can't imagine the relief. Furthermore a cold permits me to tell people I dislike to keep their distance.

On top of that I know I am losing weight. At peak production I must be evacuating half a pound of phlegm an hour. If I remember to take my handkerchief out of my pocket before I step on the scales I start thinking that two more weeks of ill-health and a really good toupé and it may not be too late for a career on the catwalk.

When a cold's at its height it takes about ten minutes to turn a freshly laundered handkerchief into an inexpressible horror. Screw it into a ball and throw it away. Well aimed it will take out a plump pigeon on the wing. Alternatively you can throw it at the wall. It will stick.

Best of all, a cold offers an excuse to visit the pharmacist, the health professional you see as rarely as possible because he failed to get into Med School. Pharmacy shelves are crammed with essentials like apple and collagen skin revitaliser in tiny pots at hilarious prices. Perhaps to give the impression of clinical cleanliness, pharmacies are always overlit. They remind me of pathology labs on television detective series, in which laconic morticians chew meatpaste sandwiches while pointing out the angle at which the blunt instrument pierced the liver.

If science has not yet discovered the cure for the common cold, someone forgot to tell the pharmacist. He devotes a whole wall to cold cures. These come in two types: aspirins and fancy aspirins.

Aspirins are just aspirins. They are cheap and plentiful.

Fancy aspirins are just aspirins too. The difference is that fancy aspirins come in bubble packs so that you get bored trying to take an overdose.

Fancy aspirins are supposed to be easy to swallow. The price isn't. But as my grandmother always used to say, a drowning man will clutch at a bubble-pack.

Every packet of fancy aspirins has a pseudo-scientific name, a monstrous advertising budget and very few pills. You pluck one from the shelves which you think you may have seen on television. You associate it with a catchy little tune. The blurb promises it will soothe the throat, clear the nose, quell the fever, stop the shakes, find you a lover, pay off the mortgage and reconcile India with Pakistan.

It also promises not to make you drowsy. I don't know why. When suffering I would like to be drowsy. Ideally I would like to be comatose.

In the end you settle for the one that describes your symptoms best. On the pavement outside the shop you read the recommended dose and double it.

The irritating thing about medicines is you never know if they're working. For one thing thing you're not sure if you're feeling better because you can't remember how you were feeling before. And if you are feeling better you don't know if it's because of the medicine. I always feel the need for a spare body to act as a control.

Regardless of any medicine a cold is like a flood. For two days the torrent rages. Then there's a week of mopping up. It's one of the rites of winter. On balance I'm pleased to have suffered one. Like all illnesses it reminds me how lovely it is to be well.

Being a tooth

If Louis Armstrong were to breeze in here right now and sing 'What A Wonderful World' I would set the dogs on him. I've got toothache.

I normally cope well with pain. I can watch a batsman being hit square in the box and hardly even wince. Indeed, I have been known to giggle. But when, as now, it's 2am and my tooth has sent me to the all-night garage for Panadol and to the cupboard for scotch and it's a hot night and moths are assaulting my face in their unnerving frantic fluttery way and the waves of pain in my tooth advance and recede like the sea, then I cut a less impressive figure.

There's nothing worse than toothache. Well, death is worse than toothache and so are most American situation comedies, but toothache can make a man desperate. It can also make a woman desperate. Dave Collier spent a year pursuing a woman called Delia. Delia was supposed to be of loose virtue but it always seemed to tighten up when Dave was around. Then, quite without warning, she leapt into his arms one evening and made smoochy noises. In the smug morning Dave asked her why the sudden change of heart. 'Toothache,' said Delia with memorable simplicity. 'I needed something to take my mind off it.'

Dave never found out if he had managed to take her mind off it because Delia ditched him that morning, but at least it proved, as Dave put it, that abscess makes the tart grow fonder.

W. H. Auden got it right about pain. When we're sick the world shrinks to the part of us that is sick. Nothing else is. Other people, as he puts it, 'are remote as plants', which is perhaps why hospital visiting is so difficult. The visitor and the patient inhabit different planets. The visitor comes from 'the common world of the uninjured' while the patient lives in the tiny world of his pain. The visitor cannot share this world, for 'who, when healthy, can become a foot?' Right now I am a tooth.

Dogs are far better at pain than we are. Injure a dog and it yelps once, then gets licking. Dog saliva seems to cure everything. It should be sold in pharmacies. I wonder if I can induce one of my dogs to lick my tooth. Perhaps I could smear the tooth with dog food.

Dogs, of course, have the advantage of being able to lick virtually every part of themselves. It's an enviable talent. Even if my saliva were as potent as theirs I wouldn't be able to cure anything except my forearms, my knees (just) and the edge of my armpits.

Toothache has one inevitable and terrible consequence. That consequence is dentistry. I am not what one would call a brave man but I have done some brave things: I have played rugby and twice I have almost made a tackle; at the agricultural show I stood quite close to a sheep for a photograph; once, near Paris, I defended a tent against a pig. When doing all these things I trembled and I sweated, but never has my back arched in terror as it does when my sweet balding dentist reaches for the drill.

Instantly I look like the Sydney Harbour Bridge. The only parts of my body touching the chair are my heels and the back of my head. Then he switches the drill on.

Its whine is like that of the midnight mosquito which dive-bombs the ear. And with that whine comes the sort of smell that haunts war veterans. It is the smell of bone-smoke.

One of my former dentists used to hire a special nurse for my appointments. She was brawny. She had made money wrestling. Her job was to pin me down with a grip learned from SAS magazines while simultaneously swabbing my incandescent forehead and battling to keep the sucky thing in my mouth. On one occasion I bit her. She loved it.

But right now, the whisky has worked its whoozy wonder. The dentist can wait; sufficient unto the day is the evil thereof. I shall try to sleep.

Postscript

I love my dentist. He forsook golf to come in on a Sunday morning. Half an hour ago I left my pain and much of my wallet in his surgery and skipped down his stairs with a heart full of daffodils.

Right now the birds are shining, the sun is singing and I am sitting at a merry Cashel Street café, sucking the deep air of liberty, smiling at the painless world and supping at a cup of the frothiest coffee. The coffee dribbles instantly from the sagging side of my mouth to the trousers below. And I just don't care.

Pull up a chair, Satchmo, the dogs are friendly.

Just walking the dogs

Somewhere along the way I seem to have got the wrong idea about massage.

For me the word conjures up the image of an elderly businessman lying on a bench in a sauna while another man attacks his back in the manner of a chef chopping onions. Then the elderly one gets up and jumps into a cold pool. Shortly afterwards he is fished out, given CPR and sent back into the business community with a spring in his ventricles.

But I have just been told that this is not massage at all; what I have described is apparently a turkish bath, thereby adding further mystique to a race whose most celebrated leader was called Kamel and who make a delight that doesn't.

My informant tells me that true massage is an altogether nicer thing. True massage apparently soothes the soul, untangles the tetraceps and induces a glow of well-being – like a sort of hands-on gin.

All of which is well and good, but in these rancid times one has to pity the true masseur. Fired with a need to knead he works his way through massage school – turn hard left between acupuncture and aromatherapy – buys a shop, a couch and a flagon of oil, erects a neon MASSAGE sign and sits with hands atwitch to wait for the knotted world to knock on his door.

And knock it does. Knock. A man enters. Knock; another man. Knock, knock, knock; man, man, man; and all too soon our rubber and pommeller realises what the readers of classified ads have known for a very long time: a massage parlour is a knocking shop.

Fifty per cent of my friends live in respectable suburbs, but the other one lives opposite a massage parlour. She tells me that on sultry summer evenings she likes to settle herself on her balcony to watch the world. A man goes by. Then he goes by again. When going by for the third time he looks furtively over his shoulder and approaches the parlour door. From aloft my friend shouts 'Oi!' The effect, she tells me, is gratifying.

She also tells me that a statistically improbable number of cars parked on her street contain dogs. These belong, she presumes, to suburban adventurers who have risen from the sofa, yawned, stretched and casually announced that they are just going to take the dog for a walk and they may be some time.

This explains, of course, how Captain Oates got his name, but it doesn't explain why the English-speaking peoples do these things so badly. In France they let the dogs in.

I went to a brothel once. In Acapulco. It was Peachy's idea. Peachy was a Canadian dwarf who had latched onto me in a bar and who was so driven by hormones he could have swum for China. When he found that I spoke a smattering of Spanish he begged me to take him whoring.

Perhaps it was the mescal but soon I found myself in the front seat of a taxi. Peachy sat calmly in the back trying not to drown in his own saliva.

'Where to?' snapped the driver.

I flicked a nervous hand. 'Up there,' I said.

We drove up there. 'Now where to?'

'Go on,' gurgled Peachy, 'ask him.'

I breathed in deeply. 'Well,' I said, 'my friend was wondering whether perhaps you knew of any houses of ill repute.'

The taxi-driver stopped the car. I reached for the door handle. The driver seized my arm. I turned to him in horror. He beamed at me and rattled off an enthusiastic catalogue of the delights of seven separate establishments.

At the wrought-iron gates of La Casa Quinta a uniformed commissionaire opened the taxi door, bowed and ushered us onto a veranda. It throbbed with cheerful people. Being a virile Anglo-Saxon I scuttled to the bar. I felt acutely awkward. Already a tall woman wearing five square inches of imitation leopard-skin was feeding Peachy grapes. Peachy was gurgling dangerously.

Meanwhile back in the Bennett psyche a mass of prudish, puritan, Anglo-Saxon neuroses were shouting at me that I was out of my depth and urging me to leave. They grew too loud to ignore. Tensing my shoulders to ward off the knives that pimps were sure to try to plunge between them, I left. Out in the courtyard the commissionaire bore down on me. He bowed, opened a taxi door and apologised profusely for my disappointment. Could he, he asked, recommend the Casa Girasol?

And that, I'm afraid, was that. The nub of the matter is that La Casa Quinta was civilised and I wasn't.

And now I have a little question. Given that prostitution has been a part of every civilised society since Noah was a sailor and that every New Zealand city already abounds in bawdy houses, is it unthinkable that we should grow up and admit it? Is it unthinkable that one day I should walk down a street in this country and behold against the sky a dirty great honest neon sign saying 'Brothel'?

It is? I thought as much. I was just asking. Forget I said it. I think I'll take the dogs for a walk.

The dinky green box

The council has given most of us a dinky green box. It is meant to prick our conscience. It is meant to make us recycle. It is a dinky green box of good intentions. But as a wiser man than I has pointed out, the road to hell is paved with dinky green boxes.

You hold a party. You wake up. You stumble through the house. It resembles The Somme in 1919. The air is rich with last night. A black leopard has sunk its claws into your skull. The chaos appals you. The carpet squelches. It reflects your soul. You feel soiled and guilty and sick.

Frantic to clean your conscience you clean the house. Into a rubbish bag goes everything. Everything. Cans by the zillion, most of them skulking behind sofas. When you bend to pick them up your brain screams, but you are driven by an urge to purge. Half-drunk bottles of cheap riesling in which cigarettes float like dead fish; whole ashtrays; shattered furniture; sleeping guests; guacamole chip dip which looks like the roof of your mouth. You try to tip it out of its bowl. It clings. You throw the whole bowl away.

You open the curtains and recoil from the sunlight like one of those fish that lives at 600 fathoms. You fling wide the windows to let today in. Deep in the bowels of your house you hear corpses stir, groan and murmur of coffee. You want them gone.

The rubbish bag in your hands threatens to burst. You carry it like guilt down the drive. By chance it is the day of the bin man's visit. The huge sin-gobbling van is rumbling down the street. Like a priest the bin-man appears before you.

'Here,' you say, handing over your sack, 'take my guilt. O shrive me, Mr Bin-man, for I have sinned.'

He grins and shoulders your dreadful burden. Just as relief begins to flood your heart, the bag clinks. 'Hallo,' says the bin-man, the grin melting from his face, 'and what have we got here? Bottles?'

'And cans and guests and guacamole and those dreadful things I've just remembered saying to Samantha and all…'

But the bin-man stops you. Like the ancient mariner he clutches your arm and points a skinny finger. You follow with your eyes. All along your street stands a line of dinky green boxes. Each is full of flattened cans, neatly bundled newspapers, strange strings of milk cartons, and, the horror of it, washed bottles.

With a stab of something nasty you realise that you too have got one of these dinky green boxes. You used it last night to cool beer.

The bin-man-priest hands you back your guilt. 'Get washing,' he says with the smug sternness of a man who holds the moral power. 'And don't let me catch you again. Or else.' And off he goes, leaving you forlorn at your gate clutching a bag of impossibility. The leopard buries its claws an inch deeper.

You do the decent thing. With the rubbish bag in the boot you drive two blocks, find a house with the curtains drawn and dump your sack of shame outside it.

But you know as you power away that the world has changed. You will hold no more parties. The generosity of your soul will shrivel. No one could wash that many bottles.

Instead, thanks to the council folly, the worst part of your nature will rise. You will join a class of person that is now spreading like meningitis through the city.

You've seen them in your own street. On bin-day they take the dog for a longer walk than usual, or they choose to go to the mall on foot. And as they go they take in the details of every dinky green box. These are the new voyeurs, the peeping Toms of refuse.

For that d.g.b. lying open for inspection at every gate is nothing less than a seedy autobiography of its owner.

One glimpse of a green label milk carton and you know you that the woman in No. 7 thinks she's fat.

The old lady beyond dotes on her cat. But nestled beside those empty cans of fancy salmon dinner are the soup-for-one and baked bean tins that sing of a self-esteem which has sunk below the x-axis.

See how the dapper gentleman at No. 21 has folded the top newspaper in his bundle to expose a completed cryptic crossword.

But above all it is the bottles that count. I know a woman who smashes her gin bottles, wraps the shards in newspaper, sellotapes the package into silence and buries it deep in her rubbish bag. For her, every bin day is a day of shame.

Furthermore the d.g.b.'s have fostered malice. The woman next door irks you. She has complained to the council about your motor-bike, your music, the parties you are not going to have any more. What could be easier than casually dumping an empty flagon of extremely cheap sherry in her d.g.b.? As you pass it later in the day you stop, shake your head and tut-tut loudly enough to alert the neighbours.

The council means well, but they do not understand. All unwit-ting they have flooded the city with vanity, meanness, prurience, malice and guilt. Take back, O Council, those dinky green boxes. Let us live.